Praise for Catalyst

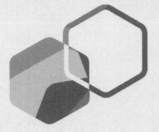

Sasha Allenby has done it again! Her unique way of communicating a powerful and compelling message, in a clear and conscious way, will inspire you to make a big difference in the world with your message. Sasha is one of my biggest catalysts for personal transformation. I'm sharing my message and inspiring thousands of people all around the world because of the content of this book. Now is the time to share what you stand for, and Sasha will give you the tools and guidance you need to stay committed to your vision.

> **Brett Moran – Author of *Wake the F#ck Up*, Former Prison Inmate, and Transformation Specialist**

This book is like a beautiful lotus that's sprung open out of thick mud. It's both realistic and highly optimistic. Sasha wisely shares how you can be a catalyst for change through her unique and powerful mix of experience and talent. If you believe in a better world, read this practical book and take action.

> **Shamash Alidina – Cofounder of the Museum of Happiness, and Author of *Mindfulness for Dummies***

What an essential, urgent primer Sasha Allenby has created! As the world seeks bold and clear leadership, it's crucial that great thinkers and activists understand the communication tools that are the foundation of real and lasting change. This book distills the techniques we need to lead effectively, whether we are new to activism, or grizzled warriors of the streets.

> **Ari Gold – Student-Oscar-Winning Film Director, Writer, and Activist**

Catalyst is a practical guide to help you understand your place in the world and how you can craft your message to have the most influence and impact possible. It supports you to tap into your life's mission and innate humane qualities. This is a refreshing resource for activists, students, community leaders and social entrepreneurs to find an impactful path of social change amid challenging times.

Samy Nemir – Writer, Activist and Founder of Queeramisú: Latinx & QPOC for Equality

Sasha Allenby guides the reader to dig into their deepest and most enduring motivations for social impact, translate them for the current political moment, and find the words to make them actionable, and therefore meaningful. A powerful book that will be magic in the hands of anyone who feels a new or renewed calling to create change.

Reva Patwardhan – Executive Coach, Podcaster + Founder of Dialogue Lab

Sasha Allenby has given us a tremendous gift with *Catalyst.* Using real world examples, she shows you how to move past surface level inspiration and into the real work that goes into creating catalytic stories that lead to lasting change. This is an essential guide for any leader looking at how they can create an impactful message. Highly recommended!

Paul Zelizer – Business Coach for Conscious Entrepreneurs and Founder of Awarepreneurs

This book really spoke to me. I want to be part of creating a better world where my girls experience more equality. This book not only made me believe that my dream is possible, but also that my contribution counts.

Katie Smith – Mother and Activist in the Women's Movement

Sasha Allenby's book is both a call to step up as the transformational leaders we can all be to make change in our communities – and a toolkit for how to shape our message and our voice so we can call others to change as we envision a better future.

Nick Jankel – Professional Speaker, Author & Leadership Expert

Catalyst

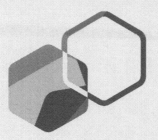

Speaking, Writing and Leading for Social Evolution

By Sasha Allenby

CATALYST

Speaking, Writing and Leading for Social Evolution

By Sasha Allenby

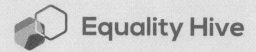

Equality Hive Publishing 2018
New York

Visit www.equalityhive.com for more details.

The opinions expressed in this book are those of the author. This book contains advice and information relating to creating a message for social change. All efforts have been made to insure the accuracy of the information contained in this book as of the date of publication. The reader takes full responsibility for their use of this information. The publisher and the author disclaim liability for any outcomes that may occur as a result of applying the methods suggested in this book.

Front cover design by Rachael Kay Albers.

Back cover photo of Sasha Allenby by Michael Cinquino.

Edited by Lois Rose.
ISBN: 978-1-7324936-0-5
Library of Congress Control Number: 2018911458
Book design by M. Abarghouei.

Dedicated to my partner, Mammad Mahmoodi. Our daily conversations in these poignant times have been a continuous inspiration for this book.

Table of Contents

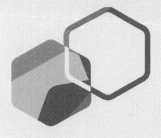

INTRODUCTION   xi

PART ONE   FOUNDATIONS OF EVOLUTIONARY LEADERSHIP   1
Chapter 1   **Creating a Vision for Our Future**   4
Chapter 2   **Social Evolution**   13

PART TWO   YOUR EVOLUTIONARY MESSAGE   27
Chapter 3   **The Purpose of Your Message**   30
Chapter 4   **Types of Messages**   52
Chapter 5   **Tone of Your Message**   73
Chapter 6   **Social Context of Your Message**   91

PART THREE   VEHICLES FOR YOUR MESSAGE   111
Chapter 7   **Speaking Out**   114
Chapter 8   **Speeches**   126
Chapter 9   **Writing**   150

PART FOUR   YOU AS A LEADER   177
Chapter 10   **Your Story**   180
Chapter 11   **Becoming a Catalyst of Change**   198
Chapter 12   **You on Your Mission**   214

CONCLUSION   229

Introduction

When the 2016 US election results were finalized, a tremor went through the world. Social media across the continents exploded with a flood of panicked responses. "This is not happening." "What does it mean for my people?" "What's going to happen to me?"

The mood was somber in Manhattan, and I was both gutted and strangely optimistic. While I shared in the collective reeling from the results of the election, I also felt that this could be the catalyst that we'd all been waiting for.

I was deeply aware of the issues that this election presented, and they also touched me personally. Living in the US with my Iranian partner, many of the challenges of xenophobia and racial hatred that were bound to follow such a racist campaign would likely affect the ones I love. In the days to come we would surely experience the aftermath on some level firsthand. Yet, despite this knowledge, I stood strong in my optimism while many around me crumbled.

I still stand strong in that optimism today.

The current socio-political climate, however challenging and painful, presents one of the most profound opportunities in history for social evolution. Although we are facing an extreme crisis of consciousness, it is also a rare chance for humanity to collectively wake up and grow. From the rubble of racism, sexism, xenophobia and homophobia, new voices are arising. Voices of power and forces for change. Many who would not have previously considered themselves to be leaders are stepping up and taking command. A new wave of activists, visionaries, change agents and luminaries are appearing, and they are coming forward like never before to ensure that the policies of prejudice and hatred do not get absorbed into the status quo.

Stepping into a Brave New World

If you are among those who are stepping up to this challenge, you are likely finding yourself in a brave new world. Maybe you are standing on the sidelines trying to figure out what your role is and how to articulate your message, or perhaps you have waded in on social media with posts and articles, showed up at demonstrations, and challenged inequality firsthand. You might have a specific message you are crafting and shaping, or be flying solo and responding to each issue as it arises. Whatever your approach, you have probably noticed that it has become very noisy out there, with a multitude of voices fighting to be heard.

This brings up some huge questions for all of us in terms of being a catalyst of impact in these uncertain times. Questions such as: How do we channel fear, anger and uncertainty into something that doesn't just add fuel to the fire, but contributes to lasting change? How do we write, speak and lead in a way that builds bridges instead of slamming doors shut? How do we use these times as a catalyst for evolution, rather than repeating more of the same? These questions require a deep commitment from us as individuals; these times require us to walk hand in hand with our own evolution and the evolution of humanity. They ask us to look at our triggers, our programs, our biases and our history and how they impact our responses. They require us to wake up, step up and lead in order to become an instigator of deeply impactful change.

Context

The question of what makes a catalytic change-maker is not just one I've been asking since the election. It's a question I've been asking since I was a young girl. My childhood was rich in a history of demonstrations, and I still remember the feelings I had when my father went to the picket lines to fight for his job in the face of Margaret Thatcher's conservative government in the UK. I started campaigning when I was eleven years old, and if there was something to stand for, you would find me there. I stood against fox hunting, I stood for women's rights, I stood for the environment, I stood against war. If something was going down, you could pretty much count on me to be there standing on the frontline.

You'll still find me standing today, for different causes, but with the same heart. Except the flavor, the tone, the resonance of how and why I stand have transformed entirely.

Many of these changes are due to the personal and professional journey I've been on for the last twenty years—a path that has led me to break down my perceptions about what really does create deep and lasting change. As well as co-authoring a bestseller that was released worldwide in multiple languages, for the past decade I've been ghostwriting for some of the leading voices in the entrepreneurial, transformational, spiritual and social impact fields, and I've helped some of the most influential people shape and craft their message so that it has the greatest impact for evolutionary change. In that time I had many revelations about how to write, speak and lead in a way that creates the greatest influence. I've developed a strong eye for the strengths—and pitfalls—of evolutionary leadership.

I've built a worldwide team of highly skilled specialists, and in this book, I'll be sharing our unique observations with you, so you can apply them to your own evolutionary message. This expertise will enable you to instantly recognize if the tone and content of your spoken or written word is going to be a force for change in the world.

So, if you've ever wondered about the impact of the way you are writing, speaking or leading; if you have ever questioned whether what you are doing is part of the solution, or creating more of the problem, this book will be presenting you with some very deep questioning that will enable you to sync your own evolutionary journey with the evolution of humanity. It will support you to carefully examine and crack open the very nature of the way you have been showing up so you can step up, contribute and lead as a catalyst for authentic and genuine change.

FOUNDATIONS OF EVOLUTIONARY LEADERSHIP

Chapter 1	Creating a Vision for Our Future	4
Chapter 2	Social Evolution	13

In Part One we'll be looking at the foundations of evolutionary leadership and identifying your vision of the kind of world that you would like to contribute to.

You'll be introduced to the social evolutionary model based upon supporting society to evolve into qualities of peace, unity, compassion and understanding. By the end of Part One you will have a clear roadmap for your own contribution as an evolutionary leader.

This first part will also lay your foundations for the rest of the book so that in Part Two you can craft your evolutionary message. In Part Three you'll be choosing the most effective vehicle for your message (whether speaking, writing or both), and in Part Four you'll deeply examine your growth as a leader.

Chapter 1
Creating a Vision for Our Future

"You may say I'm a dreamer
But I'm not the only one
I hope someday you'll join us
And the world will be as one."

John Lennon, "Imagine"

We are dawning on a new era of reality.

Although it may appear that the current social climate is strewn with challenges that are insurmountable, these issues are being brought to the surface so we can collectively transmute them. We've reached a critical point where it's the only reasonable choice that we can make.

The majority of us are strongly aware of the magnitude of the situation, and it's strikingly obvious that our solid and consistent contribution is needed in order for humanity to take a giant, evolutionary leap. And the time for that leap is now.

Great uncertainty brings a wealth of possibilities. We appear to be ending a cycle of humanity as we know it. We are also at a point where it could go either way: a spiraling of catastrophic circumstances or a profound mass awakening of consciousness that impacts the way humanity operates as a whole. Each of us has the choice to be contributing to the kind of world we want to create. Every single one of us who is alive at this point, with the power to make a choice, has the opportunity to become part of the change.

Whether you are considering impacting your community and those around you with a small local project, or you have a plan to create a shift on a global scale, there has never been a more important time for you to hear the calling and respond. For much of this book we are going to be looking at your conscious evolutionary leadership in these times. We'll be carving out your individual message of change, and ensuring that you deliver your content with a tone that can deeply impact your audience (whether that's ten people at your local community center or a one-million person readership of your book or blogpost). But before you step into leading either a small group or a significant portion of humanity, it's crucial that you be clear on the type of impact you want to make. *What kind of world are you envisioning? What are you leading others towards?* Because when you are crystal clear about the changes you stand for, when you have a detailed picture of the world you are helping to shape, then—and only then—can you lead others towards that change.

Leading Beyond Fear

Within us all lies the potential for both hope and fear.

How you relate to these qualities and navigate them within yourself will deeply impact the way that you show up as a leader. If you picture the kind of world you want to be part of and you share your vision with others, instilling hope and possibility, your leadership will have a totally different flavor than if you lead from a place of being afraid for the future of humanity or the people that you serve. It is crucial to ask yourself, *What is my core motivation as an evolutionary leader?* The answer to this question provides your foundation as an influencer. If your baseline is that you are leading others from the fear of what might be, then everything about your message—from the tone that you deliver it with, to its content, to its impact on your audience—is going to be vastly different from if you are leading based on a vision of the kind of world you want to be part of.

Social evolutionary leadership requires a commitment from you to smash up the old paradigms of misinformation and prejudice, and lead others towards greater values of compassion and equality. If you are taking others on this journey, you must be prepared to face the fear that lies within you and acknowledge the influences that hijack you on a daily basis.

Living in the technological age, much of our perspective is continuously affected by what we see and hear, moment to moment.

This not only includes the news and social media, but also the fictitious realities that we experience through film and TV. Popular fiction and the mass media play into and reinforce both our dreams and our fears. We see this in the science fiction genre, which often reflects the contrasting worlds of our hope and despair. These two worlds can be seen in utopian and dystopian fiction. Utopian fiction shows us how humanity could be if we live up to our highest ideals while dystopian fiction is where all humanity's deepest fears and darkest imaginings have come into being. These types of fiction have been part of our culture since the late nineteenth century, and they became part of popular culture in the mid-twentieth century. They have significantly risen in popularity in recent years, possibly related to the current socio-political climate.

In a dystopian world, we are presented with a warning of what could be if all of the most grotesque and self-serving aspects of humanity were allowed to prevail. It's the land of our nightmares. It's the place of our spiraling and catastrophic thinking brought into reality. Whatever we fear—whether it is advancements in science and technology, a corrupt government, or a system that disempowers us and takes away our personal choice—we can see this world made real through dystopian fiction.

Aldous Huxley's *Brave New World* is one where humans are created in test tubes and science has advanced to the point where it overrides humanity. George Orwell's *Nineteen Eighty-Four* shows a nation ruled by surveillance and controlled by an ever-present authoritarian government. Margaret Atwood's *The Handmaid's Tale* presents an infertile world where a radical religious faction has taken over and the few remaining fertile women are forced to procreate against their will. Suzanne Collins's *The Hunger Games* is a world that is divided into districts which are characterized by different class struggles, and where children are forced to fight to the death in a televised game.

These, and similar "speculative" fictions, both mirror and heighten the fears that we already have through their narrative. And when our fears are amplified in this way, they reinforce the shadows that reside within us. Living on this planet today, we have a very distinct difference from our ancestors. Through movies and television, we have consistently been exposed to the dystopian worlds of others. Most of us have witnessed these possible futures through speculative fiction novels, in science fiction movies or in TV series, and had our own shadows heightened by the mirror they create. Because of this exposure, we have different kinds of triggers to those of our ancestors and they impact our perception of reality on a daily basis. When our leaders carry out actions that are disconnected from the greater good, many of us find ourselves subconsciously recalling these images. We often picture the same spiraling catastrophic events, and we project them into our futures. We do this without realizing it, so that each time we hear a news report or collectively experience an event that goes against our core values, we picture a catastrophic outcome. If you haven't found yourself doing this yet, next time you hear a news report that triggers you emotionally, try catching yourself visualizing a dystopian future based on the images that your subconscious holds.

CHECK-IN: Identify some of the dystopian worlds you have experienced through popular fiction, TV or movies. What are your earliest memories of speculative fiction? What impression was left upon you from reading or watching this material? What impact has fiction played in reinforcing your fears of the future?

In contrast, utopian fiction shows us how humanity could be if we lived up to our highest ideals. Utopian futures present us with a world where equality and consciousness prevail and where hunger, war and disease have been eradicated. The term utopia can be used to describe a "perfect" world, and is often dismissed as idealism that isn't workable in reality. It can also be used to describe a highly desirable or nearly perfect world—and we are referring to it in this context here.

Utopian fiction shows us a world of possibility. This is seen in *Star Trek*, which presents a future humanity of sexual equality, where famine and poverty have been eradicated, where need and desire are no longer our driving forces, where racism and prejudice no longer exist: a dream of equality and higher consciousness. In *Star Trek*, the characters explore the universe, often encountering races who have yet to evolve beyond the prejudices and inequalities that we are currently working to overcome.

When I saw *Star Trek: Next Generation* in my late teens, I wanted to understand why, if we could imagine such a reality, we hadn't yet created it. *How is it that our highest minds can see a world more evolved than the one that we live in? And why aren't we already living in it?* These are questions that I've sat with for twenty-five years and although there is no simple answer, one of the conclusions I've reached is that *the vision and our actions need to match.* If we want to live in a world of equality, we need to be simultaneously picturing a possible future, and also *taking viable action steps towards that dream.*

That means our work has two components. The first is that of our imagined futures. If you have any kind of optimistic picture of a future reality, either in your area of passion or for humanity as a whole, then it likely contains some kind of ideal—a sense of how the world could be. Just as Martin Luther King's most famous speech began with "I have a dream," so too, must your foundations be based in a dream.

The second is that of practical application. When our core motivation is social evolution, we can combine our goal of creating a world where the highest qualities of humanity are engaged and fostered with our consistent effort to create that reality in small, incremental steps, whatever adversity we face in doing so. It is only by collectively acknowledging our dream, and working towards it, that we can steer humanity in the direction of greater consciousness.

A similar journey was outlined by historian Howard Zinn who wrote:[i]

To be hopeful in bad times is not just foolishly romantic. It is based on the fact that human history is a history not only of cruelty, but also of compassion, sacrifice, courage, kindness.

What we choose to emphasize in this complex history will determine our lives. If we see only the worst, it destroys our capacity to do something. If we remember those times and places—and there are so many—where people have behaved magnificently, this gives us the energy to act, and at least the possibility of sending this spinning top of a world in a different direction.

And if we do act, in however small a way, we don't have to wait for some grand utopian future. The future is an infinite succession of presents, and to live now as we think human beings should live, in defiance of all that is bad around us, is itself a marvelous victory.

This is the choice we must make as evolutionary leaders if we want to influence others to engage in expanding their view on what is possible.

CHECK-IN: What has your primary motivation been up until this point? Has it been the concern for the kind of world we will leave for our children if you don't make a significant contribution, or have you, like King, had a dream of contributing to a world of greater equality, peace and freedom?

CHAPTER SUMMARY

● We appear to be ending a cycle of humanity as we know it and seem to be at a point where it could go either way: a spiraling of catastrophic circumstances or a profound mass awakening of consciousness.

● Each of us has the choice of contributing to the kind of world we want to create.

● As a thought leader it is essential that you ask yourself: *What kind of world am I envisioning? What am I leading others towards?*

● Within us all lies the potential for both hope and fear. How you relate to these qualities and navigate them within yourself will deeply impact the way that you show up as a leader.

● You can share a dream of hope and possibility, or be afraid for the future of humanity. Whichever you choose, it will impact the way that you lead.

● You need to ask, *What is my core motivation as an evolutionary leader?*

● Popular fiction and the mass media play into and reinforce both our dreams and our fears.

● Dystopian fiction is where all humanity's deepest fears and darkest imaginings have come into being. Utopian fiction shows us how humanity could be if we live to our highest ideals.

● Most of us have had our own fears heightened by witnessing the fictitious worlds of others.

● When we talk about a utopian future, it has two components—the dream that we have and the practical application of that dream.

Chapter 2
Social Evolution

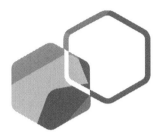

On January 28, 2017, around 5,000 protesters stood united at New York's JFK airport and chanted in unison, "Let them in."

The 'them' in the chant were numerous detainees from seven Muslim-majority countries. With a travel ban in effect overnight, US residents who were born in those countries, alongside legal travelers to the US at that time, were suddenly, and without warning, banned from entering the country. Those who had already begun their journeys were stranded in airports. Those who were due to fly were grounded.

At the protest, Jews stood alongside Muslims, with the most iconic photograph from the event showing a traditional Jewish family demonstrating alongside a traditional Muslim one, their children playing together.[i]

JFK airport was transformed. Cafés were taken over by volunteer lawyers and translators, who lined up in their hundreds to help with the cause. In a great demonstration of defiance and resistance, New York said a gigantic no to this act, and that same no was echoed across the US by a host of mayors, governors, judges, lawyers and protestors. New York Mayor Bill de Blasio condemned the ban, stating it "sends a horrible message" to those from the seven countries that "for no reason whatsoever they could be detained or even sent to their home country even though they're part of the life of the United States."[ii]

This all-out no to the travel ban was an essential act of social justice, representing the freedom of speech that is central to Western society, where individuals collectively united against an act of prejudice that might otherwise have gone unchecked. Just as the protesters in the airport were standing against the travel ban's infringement on our liberty, there are also times where we need to voice our objection, which is why acts of social justice are so valuable.

In addition to highlighting what we are not prepared to accept, there is another model, which is that of social evolution. These two models support one another and are interrelated. The social justice model stands *against* what already exists in our current paradigm, and the social evolutionary model stands *for* the kind of world that we are moving towards. In this chapter we'll explore how we can use these two models together for the greatest effect.

Justice as the Core Motivator

As issues have intensified in our current political climate, many of us have begun to talk more about social justice. Justice plays a vital role in our social structure, reinforcing moral codes that help to remind us of the difference between right and wrong. I have a deep respect for those on a social justice mission—individuals or groups who are disrupting the status quo and confronting inequality head-on with righteous anger and a passion for their cause.

The social evolutionary model builds on the social justice model, and it starts by challenging our core conditioning around the triumph of good over evil. In the West, and particularly in the US, most of the storylines for film and media focus on defeating a corrupt, masculine force. From the superhero comics brought to life on screen by Marvel, to the action and adventure movies popularized in the 80s such as *Raiders of the Lost Ark*, to the fantasy movies of *Lord of the Rings* or *Harry Potter*, to the science fiction movies of *Star Wars* and *X-Men*, to the *Transformers* or *Fast and Furious* franchises, the plot structures that we are attached to—which have been reinforced through history by the wars and conflicts that we have collectively faced, and then glamorized by Hollywood—are all tales of good prevailing over evil. We *love* the hero, and in any situation where there has been an issue or a conflict, we cannot wait to learn who they were and what they did to further the cause. It's the story that has been consistently programmed into our hearts and minds, and the one that we will most likely tune into whenever there is a crisis. Even when *Wonder Woman* recently hit our screens, and many women celebrated the shift in focus to a powerful female lead, it was still within the same patriarchal structure of defeating an evil force.

The challenge with justice is that there is always a winner and a loser. In the Hollywood version, the oppressor is defeated, the champion stands tall, and we are lulled into a false sense of security that the story ends there. However, when we try to apply this model to social justice, we fall upon some very specific blockers. In order for one group to have a victory, another group must be defeated, but unlike the Hollywood version, the story *never* ends there. Somewhere, somehow, in some way, or some form, the group that has been oppressed will likely rise again.

Moving Towards Social Evolutionary Thinking

"We learn from history that we do not learn from history."

Georg Wilhelm Friedrich Hegel

The assumption that defeating Hitler at the end of World War II was the end of Nazism was a widely accepted one. Many of us felt devastated by the most recent uprising of the Nazi movement in the US, which was magnified by the atrocities surrounding Charlottesville in 2017.

When these events occurred, elements of my life flashed before my eyes. I thought about my history lessons, the anti-Nazi movies I had seen as a child, and my trauma work with Holocaust survivors in Israel. I thought about the National Front in my hometown: the UK's version of the KKK. When I walked behind them—heads shaved with Nazi tattoos showing through the stubble of their hair—they always seemed like they were from an old, forgotten world. That they could take any kind of center stage in our current paradigm was incomprehensible. I thought about the stories of my grandparents from World War II, and my grandma—no longer living—a tough and sturdy Irish woman as wide as she was tall, who didn't suffer fools. I imagined telling her, "Gran, the Nazis are rising again." I also pictured her response. "Like *hell* they are," she would say. It didn't seem that it could be true.

Yet, it was obvious that these issues hadn't really been resolved. Instead, they changed shape. They morphed into and merged with other factions. Whether in the form of the KKK in the United States, or the British National Party in the UK, it's obvious that we haven't yet obliterated the extreme prejudices that the Nazis represented. We need a system in place for dismantling prejudice that doesn't simply rely on defeating an evil force, because if we keep trying to squash down the oppressor, they continue to rise again.

Dismantling "Us and Them"

In addition to these extremes of an endemic that we have yet to evolve beyond, there are also subtle, underlying prejudices that many of us question how to dismantle. While exploring different ways to break down the dangerous and sometimes life-threatening forms of hatred that are still prevalent in our society today, we also need to address how to work with the less visible forms of prejudice that come from the perception that there is an "us" and a "them."

I've been challenging this invisible prejudice my whole life. It started when I was eight years old when Sanjay came to town. I remember the day he arrived at our school: the only brown face in a sea of white faces. I imagine he remembers it too because 300 kids circled curiously around him on the playground on that sunny September morning. In a predominantly white town in an obscure part of northern England, Sanjay was the first non-white face that most of my schoolmates had ever seen. I can still see his shock that day as we all gathered around him, but the moment that has the greatest influence was an event that occurred several months down the line. There was a TV comedy show in the UK at that time and it featured an Indian actor who had been caricatured. Frequently, a number of the kids made a parody of one line from the show in a clichéd Indian accent, and Sanjay always laughed. I hadn't seen the show but by then, I knew the line. Once—and only once—I joined in, and when I did, something simultaneously ripped through my heart. "Sanjay's laughing with his mouth, but his eyes are sad," my eight-year-old consciousness told me, and from that moment, I saw things in a different light.

In such an isolated white town, nobody talked about racism and it wasn't a word I had heard. Despite my lack of knowledge or education, I started taking a stand. "Dad, how many friends called Jeff do you have?" I asked him one day. "Just one," he replied. "If you only have one, then why does everyone call him 'Black Jeff'?" I questioned. "We already know which Jeff he is." "That's just what we call him," my father replied. "It's just the way it is." And so began my lone campaign to challenge othering, inbuilt forms of racism, social conditioning, ignorance and prejudice—a journey that is still central to me today.

This subtle, yet all-pervading prejudice of "us and them" is not exclusive to racism: parallels can be found in all aspects of social evolution. Whether you are standing for sexual equality, gender equality, socio-economic equality, religious equality, the rights of refugees and immigrants, or those with physical challenges or disabilities, you can probably identify similarities in this theme.

In the social justice model, there are often elements of us versus them, and an identification with and a compassion for one side of the argument. As highlighted at the start of this chapter, acts of social justice are crucial and at times we need to stand against something, but *if we only stand against,* if we continue, as a society, to pitch one against another, to "other," to create an "us" and a "them," to divide and polarize, we will keep perpetuating the same issues. If we strive for a Hollywood ending where the defeated fall, then we will continue towards more of the same.

The social evolutionary model comes from being able to see the plight of both sides and moves away from pitching one against the other. When we develop compassion for both sides (even though there's usually one side we don't agree with) without condone the behavior of the other, *then* we can build a bridge. Every communication or dialogue—whether in casual conversation, on social media, in our talks and speeches, in our blogs and magazine articles, in our groups and online programs, in our books and videos—needs to be aligned with this understanding. The goal is to consistently move ourselves, and those we are influencing, out of the mindset that there is something or someone that needs to be defeated, and towards unity, compassion, connection and understanding, *while simultaneously still being prepared to take a stand against acts of prejudice or injustice as they arise.*

CHECK-IN: As you think about your contribution so far, what has the balance been between social justice and social evolution? What are your acts of justice and what are you standing against? What are your social evolutionary acts and what are you standing for? What is the balance between these two components for you and how do you see these two models working together in your role as a leader?

Social Evolutionary Leadership

As you consider your own part in these times, it's likely that the calling is strong. World events are colliding on a multitude of levels, so that any previous notion you had to make a contribution has probably magnified tenfold today.

Each time there is an act of terrorism, a mass shooting, a deepening of the refugee crisis, a racist attack or a religious confrontation, your heart probably aches even more. But it aches, not only with the collective reeling that we feel in moments such as these. It aches because you know, somewhere, somehow, that you are supposed to impact change on a profound level. You sense that you are here in these times because you are meant to move things forward.

As you do this work, we are going to be addressing your role as an influencer and the different ways you can step up and lead. It can be summarized in the following five components, which will be broken down in greater detail throughout this book:

#1 - Hearing the calling - *This is the "why" of your message.* Either somewhere inside of you there was always a sense of a profound contribution you were here to make, or the current socio-political climate has awakened this calling within you. Whether you consider it to be your destiny, your free will, or a mixture of both, the calling has been ignited, and you can no longer ignore it. It might also be that you have already been following this calling for some time, but lately it has intensified, or pulled you in a different direction.

#2 - Choosing your audience - *This is the "who" of your message.* Either you are helping people like you to shift their current paradigm or you are influencing those who see the world differently from you (breaking down their misperceptions and prejudices).

#3 - Crafting a unique message - *This is the "what" of your message.* You craft an evolutionary message—either something unique that you have to say, or something that's been said before, but you say it in a new way—and you spend time honing it so that it has the greatest impact on your audience.

#4 - Choosing your vehicle - *This is the "how" of your message.* Your skills might be suited to writing, speaking, or a mixture of both. Perhaps you excel at video or audio. Maybe your message could be more effective in short bursts on a blog or laid out sequentially in a book. You might be at your best pre-recorded or presenting live. Choosing the right vehicles to match your skill set enables you to share your message with the world with the greatest impact.

#5 - Shaping yourself as a leader - *This is you as the messenger.* You commit to consistently working on the foundations of evolutionary leadership with passion and veracity. You challenge the old models and paradigms within yourself and you break down limitations or uncover blind spots. You take your revised structures out into the world (either on a local or global scale) so that you contribute to change.

CHECK-IN: As you look at the five components of evolutionary leadership in the model above, where are you on your own journey?

● Assuming you have heard the calling to make an impactful contribution, how has that calling been played out in your daily actions?
● Who do you want to impact?

- Have you begun crafting your unique contribution and sharing it with others, or is it still in the developmental stages?
- What are your offerings in terms of speaking and writing, and which skills do you need to develop?
- What is your commitment to yourself as a leader and what blind spots are you addressing within yourself?

In the rest of this book we'll be expanding on these five components, but at this stage your main focus is awareness, so that you are able to identify your starting point.

Outcome of Operating from Evolutionary Models

When you consistently work within an evolutionary framework you are able to:

- See a bigger picture and move towards evolutionary outcomes in your chosen field
- Challenge existing paradigms while keeping both feet on the ground
- Use anger, rage and fear productively
- Build bridges with your words and actions
- Be in touch with the hope and belief that things can be different, and help others connect with their own faith in humanity
- Write, speak and lead in a way that supports others to evolve.

CHAPTER SUMMARY

● Saying no to injustice is an essential part of our evolution.

● The social justice model stands against what has gone before, with compassion for one side.

● The social evolutionary model sees the plight of both sides and moves away from pitching one against the other, in order to build bridges.

● Social evolution challenges our core programming of good over evil.

● The story of the hero has been programmed into our hearts and minds and largely comes from a patriarchal, masculine structure.

● In the Hollywood version of justice, there is a winner and a loser and that is the end of the story. In reality, the defeated rise again.

● We need to break down polarization, othering, and "us and them" if we want social equality.

● **The five components of evolutionary leadership are:**

    ● Hearing the calling - *The "why" of your message*

    ● Choosing your audience - *The "who" of your message*

    ● Crafting a unique message - *The "what" of your message*

    ● Choosing your vehicle - *The "how" of your message*

    ● Shaping yourself as a leader - *You as the messenger.*

● **Outcome of operating from evolutionary models:**

See the bigger picture / Challenge existing paradigms / Use anger productively / Build bridges / Restore faith in humanity / Lead in a way that supports evolution.

YOUR EVOLUTIONARY MESSAGE

Chapter 3	The Purpose of Your Message	30
Chapter 4	Types of Messages	52
Chapter 5	Tone of Your Message	73
Chapter 6	Social Context of Your Message	91

In Part Two we focus on crafting a message that contributes to change. We'll begin by looking at the purpose of what you are sharing, and considering the kind of impact you want to have on your audience. We'll look at how you can craft your communication to create different outcomes.

We'll also be looking at different message types. Whether you have a unique thing to say, or a unique way of saying it, you'll uncover how to identify whether your message is (i) cathartic, (ii) compassionate, (iii) visionary, (iv) a story message, or (v) leading by example.

In Part Two we'll also look at tone mastery and how to engage hope, inspiration, compassion, faith and passion in your audience. We'll uncover some of the common pitfalls with tone such as creating a message that is too dry, condescending, always angry (with no other emotion ever engaged) or unsuccessfully comic.

Finally, we'll look at the social context of your message, so that you can ensure that what you share has an impact in the current social climate.

Chapter 3
The Purpose of Your Message

"When the whole world is silent,
even one voice becomes powerful."

Malala Yousafzai [i]

Purpose is the "why" behind a message.

A well-crafted message is like an arrow that hits its target right at the center. When we construct a message, it is vital to consider the purpose of what we are sharing and its place in our long-term goal. Every time we communicate, we need to be asking, "How is this particular statement going to land with my audience and contribute to change?"

Much of what we share is a *reaction* to the current social climate, and we comment upon what is occurring based on our history, our perception and our life experience. Where we have come from, the impact that our past has on our viewpoint, and how we see the world as a result: these factors play a crucial role in our ability to see beyond the chaos of the moment and create a tidal wave of change. How we show up in the world based on what we have learned has an impact on how we contribute to a different version of reality than the one that is playing out now. If we continuously react to each given situation, moment by moment, based on the triggers of our past, we are locked in "short-term thinking" where we only consider the immediate circumstance before us. We need to shift into "long-term thinking"—which is our intention to create equality in the field that we are representing—before we share our vision of change.

That is not to say that everything we share will be peaceful or harmonious—our message can have a range of different purposes, depending on the outcome that we are looking to create. We can shape our communication to (i) disrupt, (ii) unite, (iii) call in, (iv) call out, or (v) support, and all of these are powerful in their own unique ways. This chapter will look at the purpose behind each of these types so you can skillfully forge each of your statements with intention and be a powerful catalyst for change.

(i) MESSAGES THAT DISRUPT

On December 27, 2017, Vida Movahed climbed on top of a tall, metal utility box on Enghelab Street in the center of Tehran, Iran's capital. She removed her hijab (the religious head covering that she is required to wear by law) and silently waved it on a stick. Her statement was mute but clear. She was protesting the right to choose for the women of her country.

A wave of women followed her, many of whom were imprisoned. One of the arrested was Narges Hosseini, who faced charges of "committing a sinful act," "violating public prudency," and "encouraging immorality and prostitution," and a threat of a decade of incarceration. Her defense lawyer, Nasrin Sotoudeh, said that "She objects to the forced hijab and considers it her right to protest" and that "She is not prepared to say she is sorry." Her bail was set at $135,000.[ii]

Women of all ages and abilities took to the streets to take a stand on this issue. One of the most poignant videos from this protest was of an unnamed woman, perhaps in her sixties or seventies. Stooped over a cane and barely able to walk unaided, she slowly inched her way to a snow-covered fountain in Tehran. After several attempts to climb onto the fountain, unaided, she took off her hijab, attaching it to her walking stick, and silently waved it in the breeze.

Seemingly small, individual choices such as these can become radically powerful totems of a movement, whether in a crowded street in Iran or in a packed US stadium. When Colin Kaepernick took a knee during the national anthem at an NFL game, his protest against police brutality became a symbol of revolutionary defiance among people of color—a gesture reminiscent of the move that Rosa Parks made in 1955 when she took a seat in the "white only" area of a bus, and sparked the civil rights movement.

We need disruptive messengers of this kind because they dismantle the status quo and help to shatter the popular belief systems that are keeping us from greater equality. In the same way that we can't construct a new building without demolishing the one that stood before, so we cannot build a new paradigm on top of one that is crumbling. Like a social demolition crew, the disruptors come in to blow the existing paradigms apart so that new ones can be forged.

Delivering a Disruptive Message

Disruptive messages are usually the most challenging to deliver because they always land explosively. They often have to antagonize, provoke and offend in order to get through. When you deliver a statement of this nature, it's unlikely that it will be met with a unanimous round of applause and a "Thanks for your wisdom." Instead it will incite dismay and emotional turmoil; it will cause a tidal wave of reactions, both from those who agree and those who oppose. Whatever the outcome, if you are called to be a disruptor, it's likely to be a difficult ride.

When Layla Saad wrote her powerful letter, *I Need to Talk to Women About White Supremacy (Part One)*—a piece we will look at in more detail in Chapter 9 on writing—she admits that she wasn't prepared for the backlash that followed. By the time she wrote Part Two of her letter, the first had been circulating for two months and had been viewed over 200,000 times. In the follow-up letter she wrote about the response she got to Part One:

It has been commented on, shared, criticised, referenced,

celebrated, disparaged, upheld, dragged and everything in between.

And so have I.

My words have reached far, far beyond what I could have expected, and for that I am grateful.

At the same time, I have had to process and very rapidly adjust to the sudden expansion of my business and the interest in my work. I've also had to deal with my fair share of internet trolls, misogynists, white supremacists and spiritual bypassers.

It's been quite a journey and I am still on it.[iii]

Whatever the positive long-term impact of a disruptive message, what Saad shared about the response of others can help prepare us for the possible backlash of being a disruptive messenger of this kind. Look to Kaepernick, who, at the time of writing this book, is still currently unsigned for taking a knee, and you will find a similar story. He was branded both a hero and a traitor, and the aftermath of the wave that he started can still be felt today.[iv]

Receiving a Disruptive Message

The issue with disruptive messages is that they are usually not easy to receive. They provoke defensiveness ("How could you accuse me of that?"), denial ("It doesn't exist!" / "It's all in your head!"), false allegiance ("I'm just like you." / "We are on the same team."), minimizing ("The problem isn't as big as you think it is."), patronizing ("Someday you will grow up and learn to see it differently."), bypassing ("You need to learn to think more positively and it will all go away."), and so on. This downplaying of relevant issues and the unwillingness of the intended recipient to acknowledge their part often create further aggravation. Voices of change come forward with a powerful disruptive statement—one that has been silenced for an age—and share it, only to be told to tone it down and get back in their place. This can lead to disruptors either sweetening their delivery to make it more palatable, or getting caught in an exhausting cycle of justifying what they have shared.

Crafting a Disruptive Message

One of the key factors of skillfully sharing a disruptor is *doing so within the context of long-term thinking.* When we disrupt within the context of short-term thinking, we find ourselves smashing up old paradigms without holding the vision of equality in our long-term view. A short-term disruptor can be highly inflammatory without speaking to how the swelling is going to heal. We might offend and antagonize but *then what?* Yet if we keep our intention in sight and stay connected to our goal of equality, *then and only then,* can we can consider how our statement is going to land, what the repercussions will be, and how we can prepare ourselves for our part in shifting the collective consciousness.

(ii) MESSAGES THAT UNITE

If you want to challenge someone else's point of view, one of the most profound and powerful starting points is *understanding, but not condoning, how they reached their particular perspective.* In Chapter 10 we'll look at social and personal conditioning, and how one of the keys to creating powerful and effective change is the understanding that every single limitation, every single prejudice and fear that another person holds, is a result of their own programming. When we understand that we are not working with enemies, even though they stand against us, but rather, working with *the conditioning of false beliefs* on racial, sexual, gender, religious or social programming, then our work takes on a different quality. We realize that it is the stories that our opposers have been told, usually since birth, that have caused the neural networks in their brain to fire together in such a way that they believe their narrative, misperceptions, malice and hatred to be the ultimate truth, rather than a *learned* truth. This is what we are breaking down as social evolutionaries, and understanding how to work with the prejudices of others is the starting point to influencing them.

The questions that we need to constantly ask as leaders in these fields, in every situation and with each new issue that arises are "How do we challenge prejudice without condoning a behavior or feeding the fixed viewpoints that someone holds?" "How do we understand these points of view and not meet them with our own defense?" "How do we call out their behavior without shaming them or blaming them for an inherited viewpoint?" "How do we contribute to impacting a seemingly fixed perspective?"

One of the most famous connectors is musician Daryl Davis—a person of color—who befriends members of the Ku Klux Klan. Davis's method is described as being "rooted in personal interaction," and in the documentary *Accidental Courtesy* we see Davis "collecting robes and other artifacts from friends who have left the Klan, building a collection piece by piece, story by story, person by person in hopes of eventually opening a *Museum of the Klan*."ᵛ The key to Davis's approach is that he challenged an existing perspective by first meeting his opposers where they were and then building a human connection that held compassion for their point of view, while simultaneously helping them to deconstruct it. This is the key to a message that unites. It needs to contain an element of compassion for the perspective that you are aiming to impact, and *while compassion does not condone prejudice, it understands the source of prejudice as a means to influence positive change.* We'll be looking at further tools of connection when we explore the concept of "the hook" in Chapter 11.

EXERCISE: If you are considering crafting a message that unites, what kinds of conditionings do the people or groups that you are aiming to impact have? What are their prejudiced points of view and how have they likely reached them? What do their lives look like? What issues or challenges are they currently facing?

If you worked in sales and you were considering who the receiver of your product was and what their needs were, you would fill out several profiles of your ideal 'avatars' (your potential customers) so that you could sell to them based on their needs. You can create an avatar of one or more of the people that you want to deliver your message to. This would include:

- Name
- Age
- Where they live
- Where they shop

- What their interests are
- What groups they belong to
- What they read
- Where they spend their time online
- What their issues or challenges are
- How you can relate to their issues or challenges

(This exercise can be used for any of the message types. However, it is particularly relevant for connectors because understanding your audience is key to shaping your point of influence.)

(iii) MESSAGES THAT CALL OUT

Messages that call out are ones that confront an existing social norm, but with less carnage than disruptive ones. They are used for those who have missed their own blind spot or are unconsciously prejudiced. There is not the same need for force as with a disruptive statement because the receiver does not necessarily oppose your viewpoint, and if you asked them, they would probably argue that they are not prejudiced. Your communication offers them an upgrade on a particular limitation of their perspective with the hope of shifting their point of view.

There are two ways to deliver a challenge of this nature. One approach is blunt. You deliver your call-out without any dressing.

Firm, clear and precise. The upside is you are direct without fear of the consequence. The downside is that a blunt statement still has the potential to create a tidal wave, and if you spend a significant proportion of your time dropping bombs in this way, it can take a toll on your mental state.

The other approach is to use the "sandwich method" to both connect and level with your recipient. This is a standard communication technique that has several benefits for you, the deliverer, and for the receiver too, and it often contains a suggestion or recommendation. As the deliverer you challenge a perspective, without going through as much physical and emotional distress that being blunt can cause. It gives the receiver the choice to take the upgrade without feeling the need to enter into conflict with you. Also, if you are looking for a particular outcome when you call out, you need to include a "call to action."

The following example is an interaction I had with a thought leader who invited me to speak at an online conference. In the self-help, spirituality and personal development arenas, there has been a tendency to overlook people of color as speakers—something I have been calling out for a number of years. When I was invited to present at an event where all the speakers on the list were white, I wrote the following:

(*Connecting Statement:*) Thanks for considering me as a speaker at your event. Your program looks comprehensive and I share your intention to help other authors improve the quality of their message through the written word.

(Challenging Statement:) I do have an issue, which is a deal-breaker though. I notice that, so far, everyone on the speaker list is white. Because I stand for inclusion, I wouldn't take part in or promote an event of this nature.

(Connecting Statement:) I know how much effort goes into arranging an event like this and it would be great progress to see your speaker list reflecting the changing climate of inclusion.

(Call to Action:) Are you willing to receive some recommendations of people who would create a more diverse speaker list? I can share some with you if you are.

The communication led the organizer to address her own blind spot and the program became much more diverse as a result. A blunt approach would have read, "Thanks for your invitation. I am not willing to take part in an event of this nature because you haven't addressed diversity in your speaker program," which would have been a missed opportunity to make a connection and contribute to change on this occasion.

Blunt statements do, however, have their place, and can be a powerful way to dismantle a blind spot. When Emma Watson delivered her speech on gender equality at the United Nations in

2014, she was called out for being a "white feminist." Several years before, Lola Okolosie and Chitra Nagarajan shared the following, which defines the issue of white feminism, "The feminist story belongs to all women everywhere but that is not the impression you would receive from the mainstream media, where it seems that all feminists are concerned about is a particular type of woman," and that woman was "invariably white and middle-class."[vi] The issue was eloquently summarized by Erin Canty who stated on *Upworthy* that in her speech to the UN Watson had: [vii]

. . . largely ignored the unique challenges of women of color, who must navigate the twin burdens of racism and sexism. She'd also failed to recognize and acknowledge her own privilege and the role it played not only in her personal success, but in the upholding of white supremacist and patriarchal institutions the United Kingdom and the United States are based on.

Watson was called out on the issue, and she admitted that at first, this caused a significant emotional trigger for her.

When I heard myself being called a "white feminist" I didn't understand (I suppose I proved their case in point). What was the need to define me — or anyone else for that matter — as a feminist by race? What did this mean? Was I being called racist? Was the feminist movement more fractured than I had understood? I began ... panicking.

Her immediate response of panic was a typical reaction to being called out in a blunt way, but when received in a mutually respectful manner and given some thought, blunt call-outs can lead to an awakening. After her initial reaction, Watson turned the call-out into a meaningful self-inquiry, sharing:

> It would have been more useful to spend the time asking myself questions like: What are the ways I have benefited from being white? In what ways do I support and uphold a system that is structurally racist? How do my race, class and gender affect my perspective? There seemed to be many types of feminists and feminism. But instead of seeing these differences as divisive, I could have asked whether defining them was actually empowering and bringing about better understanding. But I didn't know to ask these questions.

Watson's response was a model of how, following an initial reaction, a blunt call-out can be used to instigate change in an influential individual, which can also have a cascade effect on the audience of that influencer as a result.

EXERCISE: If you are calling others out, experiment by writing down the two different approaches. In which situations would a blunt approach be more appropriate? Where might your approach be softer?

(iv) MESSAGES THAT CALL IN

So far in this chapter we have looked at challenging the perspective of someone who sees the world differently from you, but there is another kind of communication that is equally important: one that is tailored towards someone who has a similar viewpoint to yours.

A message that calls in usually contains compassion for the audience that it touches. It is usually (but not always) crafted by a leader who has personal experience in the field they are representing, and has resolved some of their own internal conflicts or evolved a perspective that they want to share with others like them.

There are some specific factors that help frame a communication of this kind. One way to bring this into focus is looking at how we relate to fictional characters. Did you ever find yourself identifying with a fictional character? A character you could really relate to? Someone who inspired you because they were somehow like you? When a skilled fiction author is creating a character, they usually build in two types of attributes. On the one hand, the character needs to be "like their audience," complete with all the human traits, flaws and challenges that a reader can see in themselves. On the other hand, the character needs to be "not like their audience" in that through the narrative of the story they overcome a seemingly insurmountable hurdle. As a thought leader—or in any leadership role—you will benefit from displaying a combination of these attributes, particularly with those who you are calling in.

One of the essential qualities here is relatability. In the old paradigm of leadership, a leader placed themselves on a pedestal, brushing their flaws under a rug, while the audience admired a super-being and strove to be equally perfect. In the new paradigm of leadership, a thought leader is transparent about the journey they have been on to reach their current perspective. A good leader will share both their challenges and how they have overcome them, as well as their strengths and how they have been attained. They will also lay out their current issues and show how they are working through them.

You will see this in the fiction superhero too. On the one hand, we always have a hero with remarkable traits or some super skill. On the other hand, we see their challenges, often with numerous relatable traits. This is echoed throughout all types of fiction and not just in the superhero genre. If you think of Frodo in *Lord of the Rings*, Katniss Everdeen in *The Hunger Games,* or Peter Parker in *Spider-Man* you will see the same themes over and over again—the ordinary boy or girl next door who is called upon to step into their greatness, and who has to overcome one or more of their "human" traits in order to lead the way. This applies to you as a leader, particularly if you are sharing a message with others like you. Your audience needs to be clear on what your similarities and differences are so that you can model how you have navigated the path they are walking and still maintain your relatability.

Being transparent can also bring some challenges, and every great leader needs to learn to walk the line between vulnerability and oversharing. In the skillful crafting of your communication, you have to figure out if you are influencing others to change their lives or if you are merely sharing your own pain and keeping them locked in a particular viewpoint. This is an art form and the ultimate goal is sharing from beyond the pain, discussing an issue that you have resolved and made peace with but with the full understanding of the depth and complexity of the challenges it brings. If you are still experiencing a lot of emotional pain around the issues you are leading others on, you have to be acutely aware of your own triggers so that you can own them and deal with them. They may be a huge part of your teaching, but if you are only sharing from your own pain without connecting with other elements (such as hope and faith in a different future), you can end up locking your audience in the pain they are feeling. Yet when you can simultaneously hold the darkness and the light within you, then you can show your audience how to do the same.

CHECK-IN: If you are calling others in, what are the similarities and differences between you and your audience? What have you overcome, moved through or seen differently that is a point of influence for the people that you serve?

EXERCISE: Create a first rough draft of the story around how you awoke to your unique point of view. (We'll be revisiting this exercise in Chapter 10 when we look at your story, so if it feels too soon, it will be picked up again later on in more detail.)

(v) MESSAGES THAT SUPPORT

Some communications are crafted purely for support. If you are standing for disenfranchised groups such as the economically challenged, reformed convicts, refugees, domestic violence survivors, etc., you might be focused more on a practical solution than challenging an existing paradigm. A message of support is often (but not always) focused on how others can take practical action to contribute to the solution. It may encourage a contribution of time, material goods, donations or investments.

Syrian-born Wafaa Arbash founded her US-based company WorkAround as a means to support refugees from around the world to gain meaningful employment. WorkAround's aim is to be an Impact Sourcing Provider helping companies get more done for less, while giving jobs to refugees. What's unique about this statement of support is that it offers a real and tangible solution to the problem of displaced people being unable to work. One of the biggest challenges for refugees is that often they cannot get work permits in the country they are assigned to. With a tagline of "You have work needs. They need work," the company has a mission "to restore dignity to refugees through economic empowerment by connecting them to online work, allowing businesses to maximize their internal human potential while contributing to a more socially just and productive world," and a vision where "talent knows no boundaries, opportunity doesn't ask for status, and work is rewarded with fair pay." This framework not only enables refugees to work legally for fair pay, but it also serves a further core function—those in the West who have felt helpless in the face of the refugee crisis can contribute meaningful support by creating employment for refugees. So it becomes a win for all involved.

Another message of support can be seen from the online food ordering company Seamless, who ran a campaign in March 2018 to support female restaurateurs. The campaign, called RestaurantHER, raised awareness about the lack of gender equality in the food industry. Its website shared that only 7% of chefs are women and 19% of restaurants are led by women, with female chefs earning 28% less in base pay than their male counterparts, and only 33% of restaurant business being majority-owned by women. It started RestaurantHER "to champion and support restaurants, and raise awareness about inequality in the restaurant industry and help change things for the better." With the agreement that "women in culinary deserve equitable opportunities and equitable pay," it set out to bridge the gap.

A further message of support can be seen in the "It Gets Better" project—a nonprofit organization with a mission to uplift, empower and connect LGBTQ+ youth around the world.[viii] It began in 2010 when Dan Savage and his partner, Terry Miller, shared three words that gave rise to a global empowerment movement: "It gets better." It started as a widely successful social media campaign to provide hope and encouragement, expanding into a storytelling platform that helps connect LGBTQ+ youth to the communities and support that they need.

One of the key factors for a successful message of support is that if you want the audience to act, the message needs to have a viable call to action that is grounded in the real world. Whether you want your audience to give time, material goods, donations or make investments, it is essential to provide them with a means for them to convert the support into action. When my partner's brother encountered a group of students outside NYU who were selling donuts to send refugees to college, they were doing so without any plan. Every question he asked them—"How will the money reach the refugees? How many donuts do you need to sell to send one refugee to college? Do you have a registered charity or any way of ensuring the money reaches them?"—was met with blank stares. Their intentions were good, but there was no plan to convert them into meaningful actions that would contribute to change. It is therefore crucial that *messages of support have some kind of follow-through, so the support reaches those who need it.*

CHECK-IN: If you are at the early stages of crafting a message of support, consider the following:

- Who are you supporting?
- What are the challenges that they are facing that you can help them with?
- What outside help are you looking for to call others in to support (time, material goods, donations, investments, etc.)?
- What strategies will you employ to ensure that your efforts convert into tangible help?

Why Purpose is Crucial

When we don't know the purpose of our statement, we can end up being surprised by its outcome: We wanted to disrupt but we kept it too sweet and it didn't have the impact we expected. We wanted to connect but our message was so disruptive we caused a tidal wave of reactions. We wanted to call in but we didn't consider how vulnerable we were feeling and we ended up leading our audience back into their own suffering. We wanted to support but we didn't create the opportunity for meaningful action.

When we consider the purpose of our communications, we can be more intentional. If it's to disrupt, we consider its place in our long-term plan and prepare ourselves for the outcome. If it's to unite, we consider the audience that we are connecting to and what their perception is before we reach out. If we are calling others like us in, we know where our audience is and where we intend to lead them. If it's support, we follow it through with opportunities to create meaningful actions from our audience.

Always come back to what your unique contribution is. What is the "why" that is the driving force of what you are sharing, and is your statement a reflection of that "why"?

CHAPTER SUMMARY

● Purpose is crucial because it is the meaning—the "why"—behind what we share.

● If we don't consider the purpose, we can be surprised by how our statement lands.

● We need to clarify the difference between short-term thinking—which is a reaction to a current challenge—and long-term thinking—which is where our statement fits into our overall plan.

● **The five main purposes for messages are:**

● *Disrupting* - dismantling the status quo and shattering the popular beliefs that are keeping us from equality.

● *Uniting* - building a human connection that holds compassion for the audience's viewpoint, while simultaneously helping them to dismantle it.

● *Calling Out* - directly challenging an opposing viewpoint, either bluntly, or using the "sandwich method" (connector/ challenge/ connector), and if appropriate, including a call to action.

● *Calling In* - encouraging others who have a similar perspective to you in order to expand their thinking or have them act.

● *Supporting* - generating awareness and support for those who need outside help and guiding your audience to act.

Chapter 4
Types of Messages

When crack dealer and addict Brett Moran was in prison on driving charges, he carried on with his habit inside. One day in the prison library he picked up a book on Buddhism to cover up a drug deal. He started to read it and something inside him was broken open. Taking the book back to his cell, he continued reading it under the bedcovers with a flashlight, so his cellmate wouldn't see him. It was the start of his personal awakening that led him to be an authentic, down-to-earth, no-nonsense, spiritual teacher, and author of *Wake the F#ck Up*. Whether he is inspiring prisoners or everyday people with the understanding that change is possible, there is no room to argue with what he shares, because he is a living example of his own teaching.

Moran delivers a message of leading by example, which is one of a variety of message subcategories. Your message can also be cathartic, compassionate, visionary, or based on a story.

In this chapter we'll begin by looking at the two main message types—having a unique thing to say or a unique way of saying it—and continue with identifying the subcategory of your message. Understanding where what you are sharing fits in the message subcategories can enable you to be even more intentional in your communications.

TWO MAIN MESSAGE TYPES

There are two main types of messages. Either you have something unique to say or you have a brand new way of saying it.

New Thing to Say

When what you share is unique, you are saying something that has never been said before. You are the groundbreaker, the earth shaker, the visionary, the luminary. What you bring forward cuts through and smashes up the existing paradigm because it presents a statement that has yet to be heard. Your message goes out into the world and challenges how the very fabric of our current reality is held together. It tears through, cuts up, and reorders. And after its impact, a new order can be shaped.

New Way of Saying It

What you share may have been said before in a different form, but your unique fire ignites it in an entirely new way.

The combination of your history, character, and presence—in conjunction with the timing of what you share—brings forward a new and necessary perspective. The response to your unique way of saying things will be varied, but you will usually hear a range of people waking up in a way that they never have before. "I've heard this a thousand times, but I never really got it till now." *That's* the kind of response that indicates a unique way of saying something that has already been said, but that deeply impacts the current social dialogue.

FIVE SUBCATEGORIES

In addition to the two core message types, there are also a number of subcategories, and defining them will enable you to gain clarity on the sort of statement you are delivering. These are (i) cathartic, (ii) compassionate, (iii) visionary, (iv) story, and (v) leading by example. Recognizing these subcategories and using them in various situations will help you to become a master of shaping your content into different forms.

(i) Cathartic Message

PURPOSE: A cathartic message is one that allows its audience to release and transform the emotional pain and suffering they have been experiencing.

Delivering a cathartic message requires a lot of skill from a thought leader, and a delicate balance between navigating their own emotions and helping others to transcend what they have been through. When a cathartic message is delivered without this understanding, a leader can get lost in their own catharsis. When they start retelling their own story, painful emotions can be retriggered, and they are unable to either transcend their pain or guide their audience beyond suffering.

The first type of catharsis is "cathartic writing" and it is for journals and not to be shared with an audience. In Part Four we will look at how your own evolution is the foundational component for how you show up as a leader. Cathartic writing is one way to support your evolution. If your people or community have been disenfranchised or systematically silenced, if there has ever been a time in your own life or in the history of the people you represent where a voice has been suppressed, cathartic writing can support you to work through any rage or anger that may be unexpressed. On a personal level, it can be part of processing and moving beyond all the programming of lack, limitation, fear, and hopelessness. It's a way to give your subconscious a voice so that you can face the unhealed elements of yourself. As long as you are cathartically writing with the goal of purging all that is holding you back, then this kind of writing can be a useful tool for your own evolution. Cathartic writing enables you to shake up, spit out, and move beyond so that what you share with an audience is in touch with your pain, but isn't infused with suffering.

The second kind—which becomes problematic—is "pain sharing disguised as catharsis." There is a particular tone of writing or speaking that I call "sharing the pain." This is when we set out to say or write something evolutionary, something life-changing, something that is intended to lead our audience to transformation, something that is supposed to blow the lid off their current paradigm, but we have not processed or moved through what we are sharing in our personal evolution. So, instead of contributing to change for our audience, we end up sharing our own pain. This might create an emotional response in our audience. They may get some temporary relief from relating to what we have shared. However, in terms of contributing to change, *we widely miss the mark*. Our audience is ultimately not able to break out of their existing pain because we weren't able to model moving beyond ours.

The third kind is a form of "shared catharsis," and this is where we often see a profound shift in our audience. One of the most recent examples of this was the #MeToo movement, started by Tarana Burke. The *New York Times* described this campaign as "a way for users to tell their experience with sexual violence and stand in solidarity with other survivors."[i] It was particularly powerful because it not only created visibility for those who participated, but also a feeling of comradery. It was shared in more than 12 million posts and reactions in the first twenty-four hours, according to CBS News.[ii] On the surface it showed the wide variety of sexual assault survivors, but it also tapped into a uniting force that is key to a successful cathartic message. By the very phrasing—"me too"—it enabled those who came forward (and even those who weren't yet ready to step up) to feel like they were not alone, and that their experiences were both valid and not something to feel shame about. This created a shared catharsis on the issue of speaking up against sexual violence.

In summary, there are three core considerations for working with catharsis. The first is that you can use it privately in your own writing to support your evolution. The second is that you need to ensure that you don't confuse "sharing your pain" with taking your audience through a cathartic experience, and the third is that a shared cathartic experience, if delivered skillfully, can have a profound collective healing effect on your audience.

(ii) Compassionate Message

PURPOSE: Compassionate messages support your audience to feel understood. When you share with compassion, you help your audience to see that you either have had similar feelings to them in the past, or you understand how they feel.

The difference between a compassionate communication and a cathartic one is that with compassion, you don't share your message from within the pain and anger. Instead, you share it *when you have processed your own pain and anger.* You are aware of what your audience might be feeling but you don't join them there. You show them that you understand and then you direct them beyond it.

It is vital, when constructing a compassionate message, to understand the difference between sympathy, empathy, and compassion. Sympathy is a form of pity for your audience and has no place in evolutionary leadership. It is usually surrounded by an assumption that you know better or are above your audience. Empathy is where you feel the pain of your audience. It can be useful to know how your audience feels, but if you get lost in those feelings, and can't distinguish between their pain and your own, you will loop back into sharing the pain and not be able to guide them. Compassion is where you understand what your audience is feeling, but you don't join them there. Through your message, you support them to evolve beyond their fears.

A compassionate message is extremely useful for calling your audience to action. Whether you are a person of color calling others to stand for racial equality, an LGBTQ+ leader calling for sexual equality, a leader in the women's movement calling for gender equality, a leader of a particular faith calling for religious equality, a social activist calling for socio-economic equality, etc., at times you need to be able to say to your audience, "I get it. I know what you have been through. I understand where you are. *And*, if we want to create real and lasting change for ourselves and those that we work with, we need to stand together moving forward and take direct and specific action." When your audience feels heard and understood, when their own fears are acknowledged and validated, and when you are able to show them a path that leads them to action despite how they feel, you can call them into something greater.

The key to compassion is that it leads the audience to some kind of resolution or healing. To do this, a leader has to have already built trust with their audience in order to take them forward. An example of this can be seen from spiritual teacher Matt Kahn. Three years after building his YouTube channel and with some of his videos having reached over a half a million viewings, he delivered a powerfully compassionate teaching called Surviving Your Family Dynamic. Famous for his humor and upbeat teaching, and not known for sharing his own background story, he sat on a stool in front of a live audience and tore the lid off his own personal healing journey, allowing his audience to experience growth through listening.[iii] This was a compassionate message (rather than a purely cathartic one) because Kahn had healed his own relationship with the story he shared before telling it to his audience. He also had established trust with his audience; if he had told this story as a beginner teacher, it would have had a different impact.

If you are sharing a compassionate message, what are the challenges that your audience is facing? What are their fears and concerns? What parts of your own story have you moved beyond that you can share with your audience, so they know that you understand their challenges?

(iii) Visionary Message

PURPOSE: You share your vision or dream (usually at the beginning of your communication) so you can awaken your audience to what is possible.

Sharing your vision from the outset can be a powerful way to influence your audience. As a social evolutionary, your vision is your driving force, no matter what type of message you are sharing, but in a visionary statement, your ability to see a better future is *central* to what you share with your audience.

Typically, sharing a message would start with meeting your audience where they are and joining them in their pain before sharing what else is possible. The new paradigm *starts* with a vision of what's possible and then highlights the changes that need to be made in order for that vision to manifest in reality.

This "new" paradigm is actually not so original and can be seen in the genius of Martin Luther King. If you ever paused to wonder how his "I Have a Dream" speech resonated with so many, you will notice that he begins with the dream, the vision, of what is possible, and then shares the obstacles that need to be overcome for that dream to become a reality.[iv] Despite this model of excellence, for many years there has been a trend for leaders—particularly in the personal development and transformation industries, but also in other spheres of leadership—to begin their communication by first joining the audience in their challenge and then attempting to raise them up from there. The upside of this is that the audience feels met and understood. The downside is that once you start talking about a problem, you shift your audience into the suffering of it, and it can take a tremendous amount of work to help them climb out of that feeling. Yet if you start with the vision or the dream, you help them to tune into the feeling of what is possible. They can start to sense and imagine a reality beyond the current paradigm.

Having ghostwritten over thirty books, my team and I have become acutely sensitive to the power of leading with vision. For some time, we experimented with testing two samples of an introduction to a book that we were working on, both containing the same content, but one leading with the dream and the other leading with the problem. We did this numerous times. We asked a sample of readers to feedback on both examples. In most cases, putting the vision at the forefront of the message by starting a book with what's possible was preferable. Readers who experienced the visionary introduction described feeling: a sense of a calling, a feeling of lightness, an engagement of the heart, and a connection to the contents of the book. Readers who experienced the problem-focused introduction described feeling: an immediate sense of helplessness, a shutting down, a sinking of the heart, and an unwillingness to read the content that followed.

If you lead with a vision, you also need to acknowledge the challenges that your audience is facing further on in your statement. Going back to King's speech: after he shared his dream, he went on to highlight how people of color in the US were still not free, and the actions that would need to be taken to ensure the realization of his dream. If you share your future picture without acknowledging the challenges that surround it, your audience is likely to feel that you are presenting your ideas from within a bubble, that you are idealistic and not grounded in reality, and that you are disconnected from the actual problems that they face. Therefore, sharing your vision at the beginning can be a powerful way to ignite passion and possibility, but you also need to ensure that you base it in tangible and real-life actions that address current challenges and enable your dream to become a reality.

> **CHECK-IN:** If you are leading with a vision, what is the dream that you are sharing with your audience?
>
> What are the current issues and fears of your audience, and what will you share with them to show them that you understand their point of view?

(iv) Story Message

PURPOSE: Sharing the story of an individual or group so that you can lead your audience to take a specific action.

On March 5, 2018, Humans of New York founder, Brandon Stanton, started a GoFundMe campaign on behalf of the Love Army.[v] The campaign was to raise $600,000 to build houses for Rohingya refugees. In just a few days, the campaign reached its original target and by the eleventh day, it had reached over $2,000,000. What made this campaign such an astronomical success when the Rohingya refugees had barely been acknowledged by the Western world? The answer to that question is a simple one: stories. Humans of New York built an 18-million-strong following because of Stanton's ability to capture a personal story in one paragraph. He writes as though he can see into the heart of his subject and, with an accompanying photograph, he allows his audience to witness their world, whether they are on the streets of New York, Delhi,

Tehran, or in a Rohingya refugee camp. For a split second, all perceived barriers of class, religion, or race disappear, allowing one human to meet another without judgment or prejudice. For ten days, Stanton told the refugee's stories. He allowed his audience to bear witness to the atrocities they had faced. And in ten days, over 36,000 people responded with donations. The following story is an example featured on the Humans of New York Facebook page on March 5, 2018; it was accompanied by a picture of a man holding two small children *(the story contains sensitive and violent content):*[vi]

> They didn't say a word. They just started firing into the air and lighting our houses on fire. The burning began on the north side of our village, so we fled south into the forest. We walked all night through the dark. I could hear people in the forest all around me. We were too afraid to rest. When the sun began to rise, everyone panicked and started to run. I noticed two children leaning against a tree. Both of them were crying. The boy said nothing. The girl would only tell me that her mother had been killed. When I asked if they wanted to come with me, they nodded 'yes.' I'm taking care of them the best I can, but it's difficult because I already have a large family. I think they are happier now. The girl has made some friends in camp. But she still keeps asking about her mother.

In the same way that "not all superheroes wear capes," a story message of this kind differs from the other types in that it puts the subject, rather than the storyteller, at the center. If you want people to care, then stories are your most valuable currency. You can describe an issue or a problem, but if you don't create a human connection, or engage emotion, then that caring pathway will be difficult to create. If your aim is to engage the help of others, then leading with the stories of your subjects is one of the most profound ways to generate compassion from your intended audience.

There is one important caveat, though, if you are sharing a story because you are trying to lead others to take action. Your story needs to have three components presented separately. The first component is the story itself. The second is the context of the story, and the third is an instruction for action. In the campaign highlighted above, Stanton directly followed each story—divided by a dotted line—with the context for what he had shared, letting his audience know what he wanted them to do. In the case of the story above:

This week I'm sharing a series of firsthand accounts from Rohingya refugees. The Rohingya are a persecuted ethnic minority who have been violently evicted from Myanmar by Buddhist extremists. Over the past year, nearly 700,000 Rohingya have been driven from their homes and are now residing in refugee camps in Bangladesh. Their living conditions are already dire, and monsoon season is approaching. As we share their stories, we are raising money to help build inexpensive bamboo houses for these refugees. (They are currently living in plastic tents.) Bamboo houses can be built for $600 a piece, and we've raised enough for over 400 so far. Please consider donating.[vii]

The story itself needs to engage emotion (we'll be looking at how to do this further in Chapter 5 on tone). The context needs to focus mainly on the recent history of the people you are representing, as it is usually more relatable to the audience you are trying to engage to talk about what these people are going through now, rather than what they went through decades or hundreds of years ago. The call to action is usually at the end and asks for a direct contribution from the audience (anything from a financial or material contribution, to volunteering time, to signing up for a workshop or program). The combination of these three elements is crucial to success. Those with a story message will often make one of the following errors—with the result that their statement will not connect with the audience or lead to action:

1. Sharing the story without a call to action; people will be moved but they won't know how to help.
2. Sharing the context of the story, such as in the example above, but not making the human connection with the actual story or one or more individuals.

3. Asking for action or a donation without sharing the context or the personal story. For example, recently I consulted for a company that was trying to help refugees find employment, and I saw right away that they had overlooked the opportunity to share the context of the challenges that the refugees faced or the personal stories of the people they were helping. By assuming that people knew, they were missing the opportunity to create human connection.

> **EXERCISE:** If you have a story message, whose story are you telling? Even if you are focusing on the plight of a group of people, do you have one or more individual stories that you can use in order to create a human connection?
>
> What is the context of the story? The focus needs to be on the <u>recent</u> history of what the group you are representing has been through.
>
> What is the action that you want your audience to take? How will you call them into that action?

(v) Leading by Example

PURPOSE: In some cases, actions speak louder than words. When we "lead by example," instead of sharing a statement that changes the way we see and show up in the world, the messenger *is* the statement!

ConBody CEO Coss Marte was released from prison in 2013 after serving time for dealing drugs. While in prison, Marte was told that even though he was only in his early twenties, with his weight and cholesterol so high, he only had five years to live. He lost seventy pounds in six months while he was in prison and is now the CEO of New York's ConBody, a "prison-style boot camp" popular among celebrities and people from all walks of life, that exclusively employs former convicts. When Marte was asked how he had brought ConBody to life, he told *CNBC Make It*, "I never stopped pitching myself. I'd tell my story 20, 30 times a day. I'd go on the train and talk about what I do and act a fool. Whatever it took."[viii] His story, and what it represented to others about the ability to change, was the key to his success, and to building a company that supports others like him and demonstrates how social change is possible.

Another remarkable story of social change comes from Bronx-born Cardi B, who escaped poverty to become the first female rapper in nineteen years to top the charts. She started working as a stripper at the age of nineteen after getting fired from her job as a cashier, and stripping enabled her to earn enough to become financially independent and move out of an abusive relationship. Her rise to fame began through a social media storm and reality TV, which was a catalyst to her rapping career. Her plans are to keep on being an example to women, and she shared, "I just feel like I influence people because I'm like—I was practically homeless."[ix] With her unapologetic style, she inspires a generation of women to believe that they can break out of their preconceived destiny.

Jarrett Adams is also an example of someone who turned a racially motivated wrong accusation into an inspiring story. He was wrongfully accused of sexual assault at the age of seventeen and sentenced to twenty-eight years in prison. While the evidence of his white accuser was unsubstantiated, as a person of color, he was still incarcerated. He devoted his time in prison to studying law and in a *Now This* video he shared how his studying enabled him to go from saying, "Hey look, I'm innocent, let me out," to "Look, I'm innocent, this case supports my claim."[x] With help from the Wisconsin Innocence Project, his conviction was overturned. Adams walked out of prison with $32 to his name, but despite receiving no benefits or compensation, he became a lawyer and is fighting the wrongful convictions of others in his position with the New York Innocence Project. He said, "I won't stop pushing forward. I have an opportunity with each day to continue to chip away at the negative stigmas that are attached to people who go to prison, whether rightfully or wrongfully."

All the leaders above share a similar thread. The protagonist at the center of the story is the inspiration for others to move forward. By their willingness to address their own social challenges, they inspire others to do the same. Not only do their examples propel others forward, but the actions they take seek to do the same. Therefore, the one caveat if you are leading by example is that *you need to have come through a seemingly insurmountable challenge and be a model of transformation for others, and your actions in the world need to support what you share with others.*

CHECK-IN: If you are leading by example, what is the hurdle that you have overcome? What are the actions that you are carrying out in your daily life that are an inspiration to others?

Note: *you might have an inspiring story that is not your central message. If this is the case, we'll be looking at how to build this into what you are sharing in Chapter 10.*

CHAPTER SUMMARY

Two Core Types of Messages:

1. A unique thing to say - something that has never been said before
2. A new way of saying things - something that has been said before, but you share it in a brand new way.

Five Message Subcategories:

(i) Cathartic

- Allows the audience to release and transform the emotional pain and suffering they have been experiencing.
- Delivering a cathartic message requires a lot of skill from a thought leader and a delicate balance between navigating their own emotions and helping others to transcend theirs.
- A leader can get lost in their own cathartic experience and fail to guide their audience beyond their suffering.

(ii) Compassionate

- Supports the audience to feel understood and see that you either have had similar feelings to them in the past, or you know how they feel.
- The difference between a compassionate communication and a cathartic one is that with compassion, you don't share from within the pain and anger: instead, you share it *when you have processed your own pain and anger.*
- When you share with compassion, you tune into what your audience might be feeling, but you don't join them there. You show them that you understand and then you direct them beyond.

(iii) Visionary

- Sharing your vision at the start of your communication is one of the most powerful ways to influence your audience.
- The old paradigm starts with meeting your audience where they are and joining them in their pain before sharing what else is possible.

- The new paradigm starts with a vision of what is possible and then highlights the transformations and changes that need to be made in order for that vision to manifest.

(iv) Story Message

- If you want people to care, then stories are your most valuable currency.

- Story messages put the subject, rather than the storyteller, at the center of the statement.

- A story message needs three components - (a) the story itself, (b) the context of the story and (c) a call to action.

(v) Leading by Example

- On some occasions, actions speak louder than words.
- Instead of sharing a statement that changes the way we see and show up in the world, the messenger *is* the statement.
- The protagonist is the inspiration for others to move forward. By their willingness to address their own challenges, they inspire others to do the same.

Chapter 5
Tone of Your Message

Have you ever had someone react negatively to a text or email you sent and wondered what went wrong? Nine times out of ten it was because of how difficult it is to convey tone in the written form. Maybe there was a time when you found yourself confused about why you ended up in an argument based on something that you said? Again, it's likely that your tone was the problem, and not the content of what you shared.

In communication, we often put far too much emphasis on what we are saying when, in fact, tone can be *everything*.

Mastering tone is the key to artful communication in both the spoken and written word. Your tone can set your audience's heart on fire. It can also shut them down. In written communications a successful leader has to become masterful in creating mood and climate on the page. Just as a director of a movie is not only thinking of the words that the actors are saying, but also how the set, light, and music add to the ambiance of a film, so do you, too, need to consider the mood you are creating when you write. The same goes for your spoken communications—whether scripted or spontaneous. The container for what you share; the way you bring it forward; your emphasis on given words—all these are fundamental aspects that affect your impact in the world.

Difference Between Tone in the Spoken and Written Word

There are two types of tone that we are highlighting here, and developing them both is essential for your leadership journey.

1. **The tone of voice that you use to convey a spoken message** - This includes: the pace of how you speak (fast or slow), the volume (loud or soft), the energy behind your words (flat or passionate), etc. It also includes the different words that you decide to emphasize.

2. **The mood you create with your spoken or written word** - This includes your choice of words and how you arrange them to create mood or atmosphere. It's a combination of the types of words you choose—whether they are words that instill hope or fear—and the context within which you present them. *This is why clarifying intention is vital before you start writing or speaking,* because

when you know the effect that you aim to create, *then* you can start thinking about tone.

Another aspect of tone comes from the length of each sentence. If you want to create a sense of urgency, you might use more short, sharp sentences. You will probably notice at a social justice rally that speakers frequently talk in short, sharp sentences with spaces for the audience to cheer in between. If you want to take your audience on more of a journey, you might have a more deliberate and flowing style. But if you only stick with one type, your audience will easily tire. Within each communication you need to mix up your sentence length, emphasizing some points with punchy sentences, making some sentences longer so that seem to dance as they unfold.

Perhaps one of the most vital understandings about tone is that our spoken and written word convey a different feeling. One of my greatest strengths as a ghostwriter is tone, and I often have a hurdle to overcome with my clients at the start of the ghostwriting process. Most experts come to me saying that they want their spoken and written word to sound *exactly* the same. Yet the two rarely translate because the tone of the spoken word needs to be adjusted to account for the lack of intonation in the written word. You might repeat a lot of similar words in a talk, but when you do this in a blog or a book, it becomes irritating to the reader. You might sound inspiring or comic when you speak, but that may fail to translate in writing. An example of this can be seen in the work of spiritual teacher Anthony de Mello. His book *Awareness* was crafted from an eight-hour workshop that he gave. The workshop was hysterically funny, but his light, humorous and heartfelt tone did not translate to the page and, although brilliant, the book reads more like a dry, spiritual scripture with no humor whatsoever.

You can still use your spoken material for the content of your written message, and many great leaders record their lectures, talks or workshops and use their content to create their books or blog posts, but if you are doing this, ensure that what you have said translates well into writing. The reverse is also true. You might write down a script for what you want to say, but you need to ensure that the tone of that script converts into something dynamic and powerful, that you can bring to life from the page.

The Tone of You

There is often a force behind how we speak and write that is so imperceptible that it can be difficult to pinpoint. Many factors contribute—where you are on your own life journey, how congruent you are with the words you are sharing, how authentically you are living what you are teaching, as well as how much personal power you feel you have in your self-esteem, confidence, and courage to bring your statement forward.

If there are any parts of you that are conflicted about what you are sharing or if you doubt your own ability to be a catalyst for change, then the tone of your message can feel off. If you are deeply aligned with what you communicate, if your words ring true to the core of your being and you can share them with tenacity and confidence, they will have a completely different impact on your audience. This holds true even if you use *exactly the same words.*

The mood you are in will also affect your tone. It's usually advisable if you write something when you are angry to read it over again after you have settled. You might decide to post/publish/send it anyway but taking a moment between writing and publishing is always recommended, as your perspective might be impacted by your mood, and upon reflection, you might feel that what you wrote was not aligned with your long-term plan or intended outcome.

Engaging Emotions

Part of tone mastery is your ability to engage emotions. As a social evolutionary leader, you need to inspire your audience beyond their apathy, fear, or inaction. You can start a fire in their hearts that makes them feel "Yes, this is possible. We *can* do this together. I *can* play a meaningful role in the times to come." Part of your ability to ignite your audience will depend on your ability to engage their higher emotions, such as:

- Hope
- Inspiration
- Compassion
- Joy
- Peace
- Love
- Faith
- Passion

To be a catalyst for these qualities, you need to be in touch with them in yourself. To convey a vision of hope / faith in a future of greater equality / passion for your cause / inspiration to others to step up and take action, etc., it's essential to mirror these qualities in your own inner experience so that they are authentically expressed in the tone of your spoken and written word.

As we highlighted several times previously, in igniting these qualities you want to make sure you don't ignore or gloss over the more difficult emotions your audience is experiencing. If you want to foster inspiration, hope, and faith, you would also want to touch upon the anger at the injustice your audience is facing, their exhaustion from dealing with the same issues for so long, their rage that vital issues are being minimized, and all the accompanying fear and disappointment that they have encountered. You would balance out the vision of what is possible with the reality of the moment. Acknowledging and engaging with the full range of emotions in yourself is part of this. As highlighted earlier, if you only communicate from the higher emotions and don't acknowledge the weight of the issues that your audience carries in their hearts, your tone may appear too flighty and disconnected from the very challenges you are attempting to address and transform.

Rocking the Boat

Sometimes your tone needs to be blunt, because that fierceness can cut through to the hearts of your audience. Many of the social evolutionary leaders that I work with are tired of tiptoeing around the issues that they have been called to address. Leesa Renee Hall, a racial justice educator, told me, "As a black woman raised in Canada, we did not talk about race. I was told that to get ahead, I needed to get an education and work hard. Any talk of racism was met with dismissal, even scorn. I learned early that to fit in, I had to be nice and polite."

Hall helps highly sensitive leaders use expressive writing to unpack their unconscious biases. She shared, "I really didn't want to upset anyone because I was trained to stay silent about race. But I couldn't stay silent any longer. At first, my voice was unrefined. I was even accused of sounding angry. But the more I wrote, the more I realized that staying silent was a form of self-harm. It was becoming critical that I share my truth." Much of the work that Hall does with highly sensitive leaders is cathartic writing, enabling an expression and articulation from beyond their socio-cultural training.

Many of my clients in social, religious, sexual and gender contexts have echoed similar thoughts to those that Hall shared. When we are part of a group that hasn't been central to the status quo, we have often been entrained into silence and submission. If we step into a leadership role from the position of having been silenced, we often have to unpick all the socio-cultural conditionings that tell us to keep our heads down and keep quiet before we feel confident to say something that rocks the boat.

Common Pitfalls with Tone

It can also be useful to look out for the common pitfalls with tone, because without understanding what they are, you can fall into them in the spoken or written word, damaging the impact of what you are sharing.

- **Dry** - If your tone is too dry, you'll find yourself speaking or writing with no personality, void of inspiration or emotion. What you share with your audience will be more like an information dump that sends people to sleep. It won't ignite any fire or passion in your audience and it may feel like you are reading from a script or overloading your audience with facts that don't connect to their hearts.
- **Condescending** - If your tone is condescending, it will sound like you know better than anyone else. These tones accompany an idea that there is an "us" who knows better,

and a "them" who needs to learn. It will sound like you are talking down to your audience and you will alienate them from what you are sharing.

● **Angry** - We already highlighted that some "kick-ass" qualities can be essential for getting your statement across. However, it can also fall the other way. Often a tone becomes an expression of unprocessed anger. This can occur when a voice has been repressed and unheard for some time and then suddenly finds a channel for its expression. It can feel so good to be consistently angry after a lifetime of oppression, but if you get stuck there, you will be back in the sphere of generating rage without the ability to move yourself, or your audience, through it productively or create impact in the world. Anywhere you get stuck in separation and blame in your message, you will be reinforcing the challenges that your audience faces, rather than supporting them to move through their issues. If you have a ton of unprocessed rage, it can be useful to spend some time doing cathartic writing for yourself (see Chapter 4) before you attempt to share with your audience so that anger is not your only note.

● **Unsuccessfully Comic** - Sometimes a piece of well-timed humor can cut through tension like a knife. When we can laugh at some element of our current situation, however absurd it is, it takes us out of survival mode and enables us to step back, see the bigger picture and get creative in our ideas for creating change. However, comedy can be easier to imagine than it is to carry out, especially in the written word. I'm naturally lighthearted and humorous in life, but that has rarely translated well into my writing, and any attempts at comic writing so far have left me cringing on the reread. If your comedy is off, it can alienate your audience, rather than calling them in.

● **Flaky** - If you are a visionary, a luminary—someone who has an image of a more utopian future—then you need to take care how you present this to an audience. Again, if you don't ground your vision in the present, if you only focus on what might be and ignore what is, it can feel like you are presenting from within a bubble, and your audience is likely to dismiss what you say.

TONE EXERCISE

Take a section of 100 words from a blog post or a piece of text that you have written that has some kind of social evolutionary context. If you don't have a blog post, write a sample piece. Rewrite your section in the following styles, so you can be clear how it feels to express yourself in a way that is both (a) supportive and (b) unsupportive. Practice both exaggerating the following styles and adding these elements in more subtly.

● Dry – Make it so dull that it is simply a list of facts with no heart or fire.

- Condescending - Rewrite it so that it sounds like you know best.
- Angry - Write it again, but this time in a way that tunes into your anger, so that your righteousness dominates your writing.
- Comic - See if you have the skillset to add comedy into your writing. (Reread it a few days later and see if it is still funny!)
- Flaky - Rewrite it from the perspective of how you see the future could be, but with no connection to how things are at present.

This exercise might take you several weeks, but the investment in time is valuable, because by the end of the practice you will have a much clearer notion of how to master your tone to be the most effective catalyst of influence.

Style of Your Message

One other essential factor that impacts your tone is style. There are many elements to style, but one of the key ones is whether you make it formal or informal.

An informal communication is likely to be closer to your spoken voice. Depending on how you speak, it might be grammatically incorrect, with any of the colloquialisms and language adaptations that come from your upbringing or unique vocabulary.

A formal communication is more grammatically correct. It will adhere to more strict rules about grammar, vocabulary, and sentence structure.

How formal or informal your statement is will change in different situations. If you are writing a blog post, it might be more appropriate to create an informal piece that is closer to how you speak, but if you are writing a book, it is usually more advisable to write formally. On a video promoting your brand, your tone might be more formal, but on a live social media broadcast where you are ripping your heart open about something you care about, your tone might be more informal. So your tone needs to adapt, depending on your vehicle of communication.

Whether you communicate more formally or informally depends on a number of interrelated factors. They include:

- Your audience, and the desired effect of what you share
- How you present yourself in life
- Whether your statement is spoken or written
- What the current trends are and whether you intend to match them or go against them.

Audience and the desired effect of what you share

If you already have an informal speaking voice (using lots of slang, swear words, adapted grammar, etc.) and you are calling people in who are similar to you, then it is likely that you will speak or write in a way that is closer to how you yourself communicate. But if you are usually pretty informal and are trying to smash up stereotypes, build bridges and connect with others outside your usual sphere, you will need to communicate formally. If we understand that the many challenges that we are working to overcome are based upon our being entrained to notice each other's differences and not similarities, much of the work that we are doing will be to build bridges with our words. Often pulling back on our informalities (if we are usually more informal) or softening our formalities (if we are usually more formal) can help to build these bridges.

How you present yourself in life

Sometimes we will need to communicate in a different way to how we present ourselves in life. A particular speech or presentation might call for a more (or less) formal approach. It's essential that we see the difference between doing this because we understand the impact we want to have versus doing this because we are playing a role.

Having been raised in a factory town in the north of England, my dialogue is pretty informal by British standards. I built several UK-based brands before my work went international. As Northern English dialect is still often associated with lower levels of education in England, I had to gauge when to stay in my informal dialect and when to switch to a more formal tone, depending on the client or group I was working with. As I developed my brand internationally, I had to consider this further, as much of my informal dialect did not translate well, and when I moved to New York I had to make my day-to-day speaking voice slightly more formal so that people could understand me!

Adapting the formality of your tone isn't a mask that you wear. It's more an understanding that you can morph into different styles of speaking or writing to create a better connection and communication with the intended receiver of what you are sharing.

Whether your message is spoken or written

As a ghostwriter, I spend as much time working on how to translate someone's voice into the written word as I do actually writing. When writing a book, you want the material to sound like the author and to simultaneously adhere to the many publishing conventions that distinguish a book in written form. As highlighted earlier, every author needs to come to terms with the fact that their speaking voice and their writing voice may not exactly match, and one of the reasons that many self-published authors don't have the success that they desire (outside of not producing an effective marketing strategy) is that they don't take on a formal enough tone in their writing.

Current trends

If you think about Martin Luther King's speeches, you will notice that many of them were formal, often even poetic.[xxii] The opening of his "I Have a Dream" speech was extremely so: "Five score years ago, a great American, in whose symbolic shadow we stand today, signed the Emancipation Proclamation." Just as you are thinking about whether your tone should be formal or informal, you also need to consider what the current trends are and whether you want to go with them or against them.

Going with trends is sometimes the safe option. You don't want your message to sound dated or passé. However, sometimes you need to go against the tide to break through. You may find yourself swimming in a sea of informal voices and you break through with something more formal and crafted. Alternatively, everything you read sounds stuffy, tight and formal, and you break it up with an informal message that is torn straight from your heart, no polish, no gloss, just edge. So when you are creating your message, you constantly need to be thinking, "What's going on around me and do I need to stay in lane or accelerate into a different gear?" Often the choice to go formal or informal with your message will be right at the center of that choice.

It's also worth noting that this can be a deeply sensitive topic for some. In many ways, the choice to go formal or informal is linked with so much more than style. It's part of going with—or against—a socio-cultural norm that may feel counterintuitive to your message. It brings up a whole host of socio-economic issues from education to identity. However, for the purpose of this book, we always need to come back to our original intention. "What is the outcome we want to create with our message, and what is the most appropriate style to create that outcome?" If we can keep that focus in mind, then we can move beyond socio-cultural norms and remain focused on the goal at hand: to make a profound impact with our spoken or written word.

EXERCISE: FORMAL/INFORMAL

Experiment with formal/informal styles in your writing. What feels more natural to you? What is likely to have the greatest impact on your audience? Are there any situations where you will be required to write more formally than you speak, and vice versa?

CHAPTER SUMMARY

- In communicating, we often put far too much emphasis on what we are saying, when tone is *everything*.

- Two types of tone:
  - The tone of voice that you use when you speak
  - The mood you create with your spoken or written word.
- Sentence length impacts tone. Short sentences create a sense of urgency. Longer sentences take your audience on a journey. You need a mixture of both to keep your audience engaged.
- The tone of our spoken and written word differs. The same content in the spoken word will have a different tone when it is written down.
- Your own evolution will deeply impact your tone.
- If you are authentic in your teaching and writing, your words will have a different impact on your audience than if you are sharing ideas that you don't practice.
- The mood you are in will affect your tone. It is advisable to pause after you have written something and check your tone later from a different perspective.
- Part of tone mastery is your ability to engage hope / inspiration / compassion / joy / peace / love / faith / passion in your audience. You need to be in touch with these emotions within yourself to convey them.
- If you only engage these emotions and don't address the emotions that your audience is currently feeling, you may fail to make a connection.
- Sometimes we intend to rock the boat but have to work through socio-cultural conditioning that has entrained us into silence on the issue we are representing.

● Common pitfalls with tone are: too dry (information dump) / condescending (I know better) / always angry (with no other emotion ever engaged) / unsuccessfully comic (unable to engage comedy appropriately) / flaky (a vision ungrounded in the current challenges that your audience is facing).

● Choosing a formal or informal tone will vary in different contexts and is affected by: Your audience / The desired effect of what you share / How you present yourself in life / Whether your message is in the spoken or written word / What the current trends are and whether you intend to match them or go against them.

Chapter 6
Social Context of Your Message

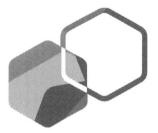

Social context is the "now" of your message.

There are many well-crafted messages that inspire faith and hope, but without social context, they have nowhere to land. What you share with your audience needs to be grounded in the intention of overcoming the challenges that surround us, the real life issues that we collectively face in this moment in time, and how we transmute and move beyond them.

If you look at the way that our current situation is presented in the media, you could be forgiven for feeling like we are spiraling into dystopia. The disparaging behavior of some of the world leaders, the inflammatory influences that their prejudices have created, the deepening divides in social equality, the environmental catastrophes, the global terrorist attacks—these are just some of the issues that we are dealing with on a day-to-day basis. How you effectively embrace and contribute to these issues is the core question of this book and how you impact the heart of these challenges with what you share is essential to your effectiveness as a catalyst.

We need to view our current climate, not in isolation, but rather, in relation to the evolution of humanity. We'll be looking at where humanity has progressed so far and the changes that are still required in order for us to experience more equality for all. We'll be asking how we engage people to care about social issues, even when it doesn't seem to concern them. We'll also be looking at how we craft a unique dialogue that speaks to this moment in time.

#1 What's going on in our current climate

There is much in our current social climate to trigger us into catastrophic thinking and we need to be aware of the many influences that lead us to fear the worst in these times. It can be helpful to mentally step back from the chaos and view our evolutionary path objectively, in terms of how far humanity has come and where our collective evolution is still needed. Social evolution does not occur in a straight line and understanding that our path will continue in long strides forward and small steps back, will enable us to stay strong in challenging times. There are two keys to understanding the nonlinear social progression of humanity. One is that this is not humanity's first collective low point and the other is that we have come further than we may realize.

(i) This is not humanity's first collective low point

Chapter 1 highlighted how many of us fear that we are spiraling into a catastrophic reality, and this fear is reflected in dystopian fiction. Dystopian fiction actually dates back to the late 1800s, which means that *it is not only in current times that we have created fear-based visions of the future.* We have been doing so for over one hundred years and our tendency has been to keep spiraling towards even more grotesque and exaggerated images of mass destruction. This understanding is crucial in our times. *This doesn't mean we bypass the work that needs to be done*, but it can be useful to gain some perspective on the fact that we have had a tendency, for some time, to collectively fear the worst outcome for humanity.

This tendency is amplified right now, and one of the possible reasons is the present world leadership—what that represents to many of us, and how it relates to evolution. We tend to want evolution to run in a straight line. If we feel that we have a progressive leadership and society is collectively evolving as a result, and then that leadership is replaced by one that seems to be moving us towards devolution, it can devastate our collective optimism. We lose our hope. We feel defeated. Then everything in our media, art, and society seems to echo the same downward spiraling vision, and collectively our faith in positive change begins to crumble.

Although our current situation feels unique, countless similar examples can be seen in the previous century. Aside from the obvious—the First and Second World Wars—there were also many moments in the twentieth century where the future of humanity seemed bleak and uncertain. In a December 2017 *Time* magazine article, "Lessons for 2018 From One of America's Most Tumultuous Years," Katie Reilly highlights one of those low points:[i]

> It was a year marked by a racially coded law-and-order campaign pitted against a fierce social-justice resistance, the unrest and defiance of a "troubled and troublesome" young generation, questions about gun control in the wake of devastating violence, and the "fear and frustration and anger" that defined a presidential election.

> That year was 1968—which saw the election of Richard Nixon; the assassinations of Martin Luther King Jr. and Robert F. Kennedy; and widespread protests against racism, sexism and the Vietnam War.

In the article, Reilly cites Jeremi Suri, an Austin University history professor and author of *The Impossible Presidency: The Rise and Fall of America's Highest Office.* Suri highlights that "while such changes might spell trouble for a political party, they've often been good for the nation long term, forcing debates about fundamental cultural disagreements." He notes, "The engine of American history is cyclical," and that "social movements don't often change minds or policies immediately, but they matter 'enormously' in the long run."

> **CHECK-IN:** Think of some of the seemingly insurmountable scenarios that you have seen in your lifetime, both on a personal and global level. What was your thinking at the time? What would you say to yourself back then, with the wisdom and knowledge you have now, and how might those words support you in your own journey or influence the audience that you serve?

I recall a low moment in the 1980s when I was a child. With Reagan and Gorbachev going head-to-head, nuclear war seemed imminent. My aunt told me that Reagan "even sleeps with his finger on the nuclear button," and my seven-year-old self would lie awake at night, taking the statement literally, terrified of what might happen if he accidentally rolled over and pressed it in his sleep! And during the day, every siren I heard would send me diving under the table, certain that nuclear war was upon us.

All too often we have been presented with scenarios such as these that have created widespread fear and made the end seem inevitable, and yet we are still standing strong today.

(ii) We have come further than we think

During my early thirties I was struck by long-term illness. My condition wasn't life-threatening, but I was severely disabled and bedridden for several years. Although this was one of the more challenging moments of my life, and at times I couldn't picture it ending, it was also one of the greatest growth periods with many awakenings and realizations, including some emotional healing that would not have occurred if I hadn't been disabled. Midway through healing I encountered an unconventional medical doctor. He told me, "Right now you are halfway up a mountain. You are constantly looking to the top of that mountain and feeling it is insurmountable. Once in a while, turn around, and notice how far you have come." These words are applicable not only to healing, but to every single social evolutionary journey that we collectively face right now. We have made monumental progress in many areas of social evolution, but we still have a significant way to travel to the top of the mountain.

If we consider global poverty, for example, the main focus used to be on absolute poverty reduction. Absolute poverty is defined as a condition where household income is below the necessary level to maintain basic living standards (of food, shelter, housing, etc.). In 1820 absolute poverty represented 94 percent of the population in the world. As of 2015, it is 9.6 percent, showing that as a whole we have made great progress in eradicating absolute poverty.[ii] However, we are still faced with a severe modern issue, which is the extreme inequality and disparity between the wealth of different socio-economic groups. The upper middle class in the US makes 69 times more than the lower income household.[iii] The Walmart CEO makes 1,200 times more than the median salary of a Walmart employee. At Live Nation Entertainment (a concert and ticketing company), its CEO makes 2,893 times more than its median employee.[iv]

Some other social evolutionary issues have changed on paper, but those changes have yet to filter into the status quo. One such issue is minority rights. We may have progressed so that people of color have equal legal rights in the US. However, statistics show that people of color are still being discriminated against, despite the changes made on paper. African Americans are incarcerated at more than five times the rate of white Americans. For drug charges the rate is six times higher (even though only 12.5 percent of illicit drug users are African American)[v], and black Americans are killed by police at a far higher rate than any other race (representing 31 percent of police killings yet only 13 percent of the US population).[vi] These statistics do not even begin to address the increased violence faced by people of color in everyday situations.

Our duty as social evolutionary leaders is to break down the assumptions that are embedded in the status quo. In the case of racial equality, the shift of focus has moved from securing equal legal rights for people of color, to eradicating commonly held prejudices so that those equal rights are applied in everyday situations. Similar changes are being called for in every area of social evolution. The law may change to support equality, but until this is reflected in the status quo, we still have work to do.

CHECK-IN: What is the history of the arena of social evolution that you are impacting? What is the progress that has been made so far? What areas are still evolving? Gaining clarity on the milestones can form an essential part of your messaging, because in the times when you are giving your audience hope and faith in a different future, using facts to highlight the progress made can be a vital tool for creating optimism.

#2 How we engage people to care about what's going on (even when it doesn't seem to concern them)

"When we take advantage of a capitalist system, we also have to take responsibility for its shortcomings. When the system does not support the vulnerable members of our society, we have to choose to take it upon ourselves to step up and help." – Mammad Mahmoodi

You can tell a lot about a society from how they take care of their sick, poor and elderly.

When I emigrated from the UK to the US, it was an eye-opener to discover the extent of the socio-economic imbalance. London has a similar population to New York, yet London's homeless population is around 1,140 on any given night[vii] compared to more than 60,000 in Manhattan alone.[viii] New York's homeless include those with disabilities, war veterans, and even pregnant women or parents with children, which from my own socio-cultural perspective, was a lot to comprehend. If New York is one of the three wealthiest cities in the world (the others are London and Tokyo), then why is the gap between those who prosper and those who barely survive so incredibly vast?[ix]

This raises an important social question. When we witness a vast array of people that potentially need the help of those in stronger positions to survive or prosper, how do we engage those who aren't directly affected to care? (And although this is a question about socio-economic issues, how we engage others to care about issues that aren't on their agenda is applicable to all aspects of social evolution.)

If we look around us, it is easy to focus on the maldistribution of wealth, particularly in a capitalist society. When I share that, according to the Borgen Project, it would take 30 billion dollars a year to end world hunger, most people's first response is to look to those who have the greatest proportion of the wealth to fix the problem.[x]

- Jeff Bezos of Amazon has a net worth of $90.6 billion.[xi]
- Bill Gates has a net worth of $90 billion.[xii]
- Amancio Ortega, self-made Spanish billionaire, has a net worth of $83.2 billion.[xiii]
- Warren Buffett, Berkshire Hathaway CEO, has a net worth of $74.3 billion.[xiv]

It's easy to put solving the world hunger crisis on the billionaires of the world, and indeed it seems that individually or collectively, they could do so—and there is a commonly held belief that those with the greatest power should take the most responsibility. It's equally easy to put responsibility on the government. For example, the US defense budget is $737 billion per year. Just a fraction of this could potentially solve the world hunger crisis, let alone address the problems of the hungry in the US, where, in 2016, 41 million people struggled with hunger issues.[xv]

However, when we blame those with power for the shortfalls of society, we simultaneously give our own power away, because what we do individually is equally important. As social evolutionaries, we are not simply looking outside of ourselves to point blame at the government or the unfair distribution of wealth. Instead we are asking questions, such as "What can we do on the ground?" "What is our role in socially impacting these challenges?" "How do we rally the people that we influence to make small, but vital differences at a grassroots level?"

Many of our audience may not consider how a small shift in their daily choices could have a profound impact—if we could encourage larger groups of people to make smaller shifts. Yet when we look at our mass expenditure, we can see where some of the challenges lie:

- The total pet industry expenditures for 2015 in the US was $60.59 billion[xvi] and globally in 2016 it topped over $100 billion worldwide.[xvii]
- Beauty is a $445 billion industry.[xviii]
- The global fashion industry is valued at $3 trillion.[xix]
- On Cyber Monday, in 2017, Americans spent $6.59 billion *in one day.*[xx]

These figures help us to understand that society has far more financial power to collectively make an impact than we might realize, and that much of our work is about engaging people down on the ground at the grassroots level, rather than waiting for changes to come from above. According to economist Mammad Mahmoodi, if each American gave away 0.16 percent of their annual income, it would eliminate 100 percent of hunger in the world. That would equate to one dollar for each $620 dollars of income.

A powerful example of social responsibility is modeled in the Muslim community, where 20 percent of earnings are given to those with socio-economic challenges.[xxi] This is a mandatory condition (it is one of the pillars of the Quran) and one that serves to create more balance in society. A particular challenge in a capitalist society, where we have been trained to focus on the growth of the individual over the growth of the society is: How do we engage people to make choices that show care to those who need it, without making them mandatory and shaming them into that choice? And most importantly, how do we authentically model those choices to the audience that we are influencing so that they can engage in socially beneficial choices without being shamed or blamed into doing so?

CHECK-IN: If you look at your own choices, are there any incremental changes that you could make that would be a model of change for your audience?

If you want to engage your audience to take action, what are their commonly held beliefs that you need to break down before you can encourage them to engage?

#3 Timing our message so that what we share is current and relevant

In 2006, Rhonda Byrne released *The Secret*, a book that has since been translated into 50 languages and sold 20 million copies worldwide.[xxii] I've frequently been approached by potential authors who have asked me to "write the next *Secret*." I've always turned the offer down. *The Secret* was a message for its time. The message—based on the Law of Attraction, which suggests that what we focus on, we create—had already been collectively absorbed through Byrne's book and accompanying film. It had its moment, a window in history where it was prevalent and impactful, and then the moment passed and did not need to be recreated. You want to make sure you are focusing your energy on a message that is going to have the greatest impact in *this* moment—that what you share is current, relevant and catalytic.

At the same time, you want to ensure that what you say is not clichéd. Gandhi's "Be the change you want to see in the world," is one that became overused in the last decade. When Gandhi shared it, he *was* being the change, but many who repeated it afterwards were doing so conceptually without putting it into practice. It lost its power and its impact because it was used over and over again by emerging influences without authentic application.

CHECK-IN: What makes your message current? How is it grounded in the challenges of our times?

Are there any elements of your message that feel clichéd or tired? Maybe there are phrases that you are repeating from other thought leaders that you have not uniquely crafted or made your own. How can you reword what you say in order to have more ownership of it?

CHAPTER SUMMARY

- Social context is the 'now' of your message.
- What you share with your audience needs to be grounded in the intention of overcoming the challenges that surround us.
- Without social context, what you share will not connect to the wider web of humanity or have the power to create impact in the current social arena.
- We need to understand our current climate, not in isolation, but rather, in relation to the evolution of humanity.
- There is much in our current social climate to trigger us into catastrophic thinking. It can be helpful to mentally step back from the chaos and view our evolutionary path objectively.
- This is not humanity's first collective low point.
- Although this current situation feels unique, countless

similar examples can be seen in the previous century.

● We have come further than we think. We still have much progress to make, but there are many identifying markers that are indicators of our evolution.

● When we witness a vast array of people that potentially need the help of those in stronger positions to survive or prosper, we need to consistently ask how we engage those who aren't directly affected to care.

● When we blame those with power for the shortfalls of society, we simultaneously give our own power away.

● Many of our audience may not consider how a small shift in their daily choices could have a profound impact.

● Society has far more financial power to collectively make an impact than we realize, and much of our work is about engaging people down on the ground at the grassroots level.

● We need to ensure that the timing of our message is current and relevant.

EXERCISE: PART TWO ROUNDUP

In Part Two we've covered four main considerations for your message:

PURPOSE:
● Disrupt - cut through an existing paradigm
● Unite - make a connection to others who may not see the world the same as you

- Call out - question a blind spot of someone who has a similar view to you
- Call in - invite those who have a similar point of view as you to unite and take action
- Support - offer practical solutions to a particular issue or group.

TYPE:

You will either have (i) a unique thing to say or (ii) a brand new way of saying something that has already been said. What you share or how you share it might fall into one of the following five subcategories:

- Cathartic - Audience releases pain
- Compassionate - Audience feels understood
- Visionary - Starts with vision and then highlights the obstacles
- Story - the subject, rather than the storyteller, is at the center of the message
- Leading by Example - the messenger *is* the message.

TONE:

- Engage hope / inspiration / compassion / joy / peace / love / faith / passion in your audience, and at the same time, connect with the challenges that your audience is facing.

• Common pitfalls with tone are: too dry (information dump) / condescending (I know better) / always angry (with no other emotion ever engaged) / unsuccessfully comic (unable to engage comedy appropriately) / flaky (a vision ungrounded in the current challenges that your audience is facing).

• Choosing a formal or informal tone will vary in different contexts and is affected by: Your audience, and the desired effect of your message / How you present yourself in life / Whether your message is spoken or written / What the current trends are / Whether you intend to match the current trends or go against them.

SOCIAL CONTEXT:

• Consider your message in relation to everything that is occurring in our current social climate.

• Make sure your timing is precise.

Now spend some time crafting your unique message. Write it in:

1. fifty words
2. one paragraph
3. one page

Discuss it with members of your target audience, knowledgeable friends or business associates.

This exercise will likely take you several weeks or more and it is crucial to keep defining and refining it, because what you create here is the heartbeat of your work going forward.

VEHICLES
FOR
YOUR MESSAGE

Chapter 7	Speaking Out	114
Chapter 8	Speeches	126
Chapter 9	Writing	150

In Part Three we focus on speaking and writing as the main vehicles for your message. We look at the different approaches to speaking out against acts of prejudice and carefully crafting a speech for an audience. We also look at different writing styles, so you can begin to see thought leaders from contrasting social evolutionary fields communicating powerfully through the written word.

Chapter 7
Speaking Out

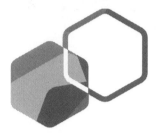

There are times when you are going to be called to deliver your message spontaneously.

Whether someone confronts you in the street, in a social setting, at an event, or on a live broadcast, there will likely be moments that you will need to lead "right out of the gate" with the message that you share. When you know what your message is, and you have considered the prejudices or misperceptions that you might face, you will be more effective in sharing a spontaneous response than if you haven't prepared in advance.

In this chapter we are going to look at three powerful examples of how xenophobia, racism, and Islamophobia were tackled in live broadcasts and events, and we'll follow them up with a short breakdown of the evolutionary qualities that each individual modeled with their response. By the end of this chapter you will have a clear outline of the kinds of prejudices you might face, and your planned responses to them, so that you are less likely to get blindsided and can stand strong in what you are sharing, even in the face of conflict.

Hoda Katebi - Speaking Out Against Xenophobia

When Iranian-American fashion blogger Hoda Katebi appeared on Chicago's WGN-TV to talk about her book *Tehran Streetstyle*, the interview began in a fairly predictable manner.[i] She was asked about her experiences growing up in a predominantly white, conservative state, and some questions around the fashion style in Iran. However, the interview took a dramatic turn when one of the presenters suddenly landed her with an incongruous question about Iran's nuclear arsenal. "Some of our viewers may say we cannot trust Iran," host Larry Potash told her, and then asked, "What are your thoughts?"

Katebi came back strong. "I don't think we can trust *this* country [the US]." She told the presenters, "I am a pacifist, I don't believe in violence. But also, when we look at the legacy of imperialism and colonization in the Middle East and we see the legacy of this country and all of the violence that it has not only created— but also created the capacity for—a lot of these weapons in the Middle East are completely brought in by the United States."

Katebi went on to highlight how it is vital that we "look beyond these simple narratives that we're told, whether it's about Muslim women or the legacy of the country, knowing that this country was literally built on the backs of Black slaves and after the genocide of indigenous people. I think there is a lot we can be proud about," she said, "but I think we should not let that blindside us to the realities of the situation."

Breaking Down Katebi's Narrative

Message Type: Call-Out
Tone: Strong, clear, precise, unwavering

Katebi's tone was measured and her response was non-reactive. She didn't let herself be thrown off by the current narrative on Muslim countries in the US, and her argument was well-rounded because it created a greater context for the accusations that were placed upon her and her country, and gave the audience a chance to see things from a holistic, rather than myopic, perspective.

Afua Hirsch - Dealing with Racism Deniers

When Afua Hirsch appeared on the UK Sky News show *The Pledge* to talk about racism in the UK, she presented with an all-white panel, featuring several "racism deniers."[ii]

In response to a comment about racism from one of the presenters, Hirsch asked, "Do you think as a white person in a society where the majority of people are white, you have a good understanding of the ways in which race affects people psychologically? Because when you say you 'don't see racism'," speaking directly to one of the co-hosts, Michelle, she continued, "I wouldn't expect you to see it [...] because it's not your experience. I wouldn't imagine you get 'othered' regularly. I wouldn't imagine that you carry and experience the baggage of being in a country that colonized on a white supremacist ideology, other countries, for 400 years."

Other white panelists attempted to belittle her assertions: "Life's moved on, Afua." But she came back with a quick response, "And it's very easy to say that if you don't experience it."

Another panelist asked her, "Do you feel it?" and she replied, "I have experienced it. I have just written a book about the experience, and not as a victim."

"But how often, Afua? Seriously, how often?" she was asked, in a tone that appeared to minimize what she was sharing.

"As a daily experience," she replied, and this was met with a question from another presenter who clearly doubted her experience was actually daily. She went on to clarify, "Not overt racism but acts of othering, [...] micro-aggressions, subtle prejudice that often comes from very well-meaning people, who mean no harm, who don't even see themselves as racist."

Her co-presenter talked over her: "So therefore it's not racism. If it's well-intentioned, it's not racism," and with grace, she again handled this misconception that she should accept institutional racism.

"One of the problems is the idea that 'I don't see race.' You are distancing yourself from a history where people judged each other on race and prejudiced others based on their race. [...] When you say you don't see something, you are blinding yourself to reality. We live in a world where racial injustice is a structural part of our reality so if you choose not to see it you are blinding yourself to it."

As the panel went on talking over her, she continued, firm, calm and measured, "Secondly my heritage as a black person is not something I want you to be blind to. It's part of who I am. So by saying you don't see it, you are blinding yourself to something that I see as positive." She added that this still made her question whether people see race as a negative thing when they think it is better not to see it.

Breaking Down Hirsch's Narrative

Message Type: Call-Out
Tone: Strong, firm, assertive, unwavering

Like Katebi in the example before this one, it is obvious that Hirsch was prepared with her responses. Some of her core strengths included sticking with her message in the face of doubters and deniers. She did not make enemies of her fellow presenters, despite their misperceptions. She attempted to meet them where they were and explain to them that their well-meaning responses were still laced with prejudice. Her speech was a calm and centered response to breaking down some of the more subtle and insidious prejudices that lie beneath a well-meaning exterior.

Jagmeet Singh - Meeting Islamophobia with Love

At a public meet-and-greet session, Canadian political candidate Jagmeet Singh was interrupted by an angry woman who accused him of supporting "sharia law." [iii]

Singh, who is Sikh, allowed her to express her anger before asserting that he would not allow the meeting to be "intimidated by hate."

"We don't want hatred to ruin a positive event. So let's show people how we treat people with love," he said to his audience, as he encouraged them to applaud.

"When is *your* sharia going to end?" the woman said (she was actually referring to a part of Islamic, rather than Sikh, law).

Singh's supporters attempted to interject and usher the woman offstage, but she threatened to call in the police.

Singh then spoke directly to the audience: "What do we believe in? Love and courage. We believe in an inclusive Canada where no one is left behind. We believe in building a Canada that ensures that there is economic justice for everybody."

She continued to confront him, pointing in his face and asking, "When is your sharia going to stop?"

He then addressed her directly, "We welcome you. We love you. We support you. We believe in your rights..."

While he spoke directly to her, the crowd chanted the slogan "Love and Courage" over and over. This was the slogan that Singh used in his leadership campaign.

After several minutes, the woman walked away.

"It's not a problem. We can deal with it. There's going to be other obstacles we're going to face, and we're going to face them with what? With *love and courage,*" he said, after explaining to the crowd that as a brown-skinned man wearing a turban, this type of confrontation was not something new to him—he had encountered many situations like this before.

After the event, Singh was asked why he didn't immediately let the woman know that he was Sikh, and not Muslim.[iv] He responded, "Many people have commented that I could have just said I'm not Muslim. In fact, many have clarified that I'm actually Sikh," he said. "While I'm proud of who I am, I purposely didn't go down that road because it suggests their hate would be ok if I was Muslim. We all know it's not."

"I didn't answer the question because my response to Islamophobia has never been 'I'm not Muslim.' It has always been and will be that 'hate is wrong.'"

Breaking Down Singh's Response

Message Type: Leading by example/ Message that unites
Tone: Love, acceptance, connection

Singh's speech represents the actions of a true evolutionary because he modeled one of the biggest challenges that all of us face: how to remain in a state of love in the face of the prejudice of another. This was further exemplified by his choice not to highlight that he was Sikh and that his accuser was referring to

Muslim law. He not only didn't address the prejudice projected onto him in that moment—he also allowed his actions and responses to dismantle generalized hate and misperception, and in doing so, he left no space for Islamophobia to spread further.

PREPARING FOR SPONTANEOUS SPEECHES

Although in the examples above we saw thought leaders responding articulately and with great precision in the moment, they didn't get there overnight. It is imperative to prepare for possible confrontations to give yourself the best chance of remaining on point in a situation of this nature.

In Part Four when we will look at you as a leader, we'll be examining your triggers and what is most likely to send you into anger, fear, separation, and other strong emotional responses. It is useful to know the kinds of situations that trigger you, particularly if you are putting yourself in scenarios where you are likely to encounter prejudice. How you handle it and respond accordingly is a growth curve that is shared with all social evolutionaries.

In the early days of my relationship with my Iranian partner in the US, I didn't handle incidents of xenophobia—that were directed towards him—very effectively. On several occasions I responded explosively. Another time, when an insidious comment was made, I froze in shock and was unable to respond. My partner was able to navigate these comments with far more ease than I did, and with his resilient approach, and his insistence not to let someone else's perception of him hijack his day, I learned a lot as he modeled how to be in the world without taking things so personally. Something I also realized was this: because of my tendency to get so strongly triggered into defending him in these moments, it was essential for me to prepare possible responses that were more aligned with my values than shouting or freezing.

I want to take a moment to acknowledge the part-time nature of my experiences in this, and similar situations. In one sense, my life path has afforded me a cross-section of exposures to different prejudices. I grew up in a strongly patriarchal household in a socially deprived area of the UK where women were still seen as inferior. For a while I lived in the Middle East and was on the receiving end of religious prejudice. For several years I was severely disabled and unable to walk. And I recognize the temporary nature of all of the challenges that I faced. I had the intellectual resources to move out of a socially deprived and overwhelmingly patriarchal setting. I could have left the Middle East at any time I chose. I healed from the disabling health condition. I did not ever experience long-term and persistent prejudices from which there is no release.

A similar sentiment was shared recently at a soup kitchen in Manhattan, when one of the clients, Clive, highlighted to my partner how frustrated he was about a project that encouraged people to "Sleep rough for one night so they can better understand homelessness." Although these projects are designed to build empathy and raise awareness, Clive expressed that for him, the real challenge of being homeless was the relentless, day-to-day grind of living that could not be encapsulated in one night's sleeping outside.

This relates to you as a social evolutionary leader because the depth to which you have felt the pain in your soul of the social inequality you are working to overcome, the degree to which it has felt relentless to you, and the extent to which it triggers you emotionally, will impact how much you need to prepare for the responses of others. As you take your message out into a wider sphere, particularly if what you are sharing is a direct challenge to a popularly held point of view that affects you directly, and one that you have been standing against for a lifetime, it is useful to know your habitual responses when prejudice arises. Do you fight, run away, or freeze? Knowing how you react and being prepared in advance for such an event can mean you are more likely to respond in a way that builds your message, modeling alternative ways of responding. (We'll be breaking this down further in Chapter 10 on Your Story.) You need a ton of self-compassion if the issue you are dealing with weighs heavy on your soul and feels relentless, because remaining articulate in the face of prejudice can have a huge learning curve.

THINKING POINT: What kinds of prejudices and misperceptions are you likely to face in one-to-one communication/ in interviews/ when giving talks or speeches? Imagining the possible different scenarios, what is your intended approach? What preparations do you need to make in order to give yourself the best chance of responding in a way that supports your message?

CHAPTER SUMMARY

• There are times you are going to be called to deliver your message spontaneously.

• When you know what your message is, and you have considered the prejudices or misperceptions that you are likely to face, you will usually be more effective when sharing a spontaneous response.

• You will probably need a lot of careful preparation if you are dealing with an issue of prejudice that you have spent a lifetime navigating.

• The depth to which you have felt the pain in your soul of the social inequality you are working to overcome, the degree to which it has felt relentless to you, and the extent to which it triggers you emotionally, will impact how much you need to prepare for the responses of others.

Chapter 8
Speeches

Did you know that Obama had a speechwriter?

Although we tend to think of many of the great speeches of our modern times as being spontaneous, most of them were carefully crafted in advance.

The fact that the larger majority of the population can express themselves through speech is both an advantage and a drawback in leadership. On one side, we can paint a canvas with our spoken word. We can cut through, shake up, elevate, and stimulate. On the other side, oftentimes, because speaking is a right that most of us have, we don't always consider the difference between a speech that comes naturally and one that we have prepared. Often we assume that we should automatically know what we should say in every circumstance. Alternatively, if we are a planner, we end up over-rehearsing our speech, sounding mechanical and void of energy.

As we highlighted in the chapter before, some of your speeches will be spontaneous, and arise from you having carefully crafted your message. Others will be more planned.

If you are crafting your speeches, you need to consider how to keep them alive. Whether you are delivering them in front of a live audience or recording them on audio or video, it's essential that you master the art of organic speaking so that you don't sound like you are reading from a script. However, in this chapter we'll be focusing less on what makes a great speaker and more on the quality of the words that you use. Depending on whether you speak it or write it, every single word will feel different. The same word can have a variety of meanings, depending on how you express it, punctuate it, emphasize it, and so on. We'll be looking at some of the most powerful social evolutionary speeches of recent years and breaking them down so that you can get clear on the qualities that make an impactful speech that contributes to change.

We'll begin to build on some of the considerations that we touched upon earlier in this book. In Chapter 3, we looked at the purpose of your messages including those that disrupt, unite, call in, call out and support. In this chapter we will see those in action, so that you can begin to craft your speech with your intended effect. In Chapter 5 we also looked at tone mastery. Each of your messages is going to have a specific tone, and this tone goes beyond the sound of your voice—it extends into the atmosphere you've created with the words that you've spoken. We will be looking at how the various featured thought leaders engaged hope, compassion, optimism and faith, etc. with their tone so that you can hone your ability to take your audience on an emotional journey that leads them to your vision.

Before we break down the talks in this chapter, one essential consideration is that all the speeches you'll see below were spoken out loud. Often when a speech is translated to paper, some essential components that existed because of the speaker's presence and tone of voice are lost. It is therefore recommended that you view the recordings of these speeches, so that you experience them in action. *(See www.equalityhive. com/book-resources/ for the links.)*

SPEECHES THAT CALL OUT

Reminder: A message that calls out is one that directly challenges an opposing point of view.

Emma González Speech

On March 24, 2018, hundreds of thousands of people from all walks of life stood before Emma González as she delivered her chilling anti-gun speech at the *March for Our Lives* rally in Washington.[i]

"Six minutes and about twenty seconds. In a little over six minutes, seventeen of our friends were taken from us, fifteen were injured, and everyone, absolutely everyone, in the Douglas Community was forever altered," she told the crowd, who chanted her name in support as she wiped tears from her face.

"Everyone who was there understands. Everyone who has been touched by the cold grip of gun violence understands. [...] No one could comprehend the devastating aftermath or how far this reached or where this could go. For those who still can't comprehend because they refuse to, I'll tell you where it went. Right into the ground, six feet deep."

She went on to state how "Six minutes and twenty seconds with an AR-15" had taken away the gift of life from every one of her classmates who was lost. "Six minutes and twenty seconds [...] and my friend Carmen would never complain to me about piano practice. Aaron Feis would never call Kira, "Miss Sunshine." Alex Schachter would never walk into school with his brother Ryan. Scott Beigel would never joke around with Cameron at camp. Helena Ramsey would never hang out after school with Max. Gina Montalto would never wave to her friend Liam at lunch. Joaquin Oliver would never play basketball with Sam or Dylan. Alaina Petty would never. Cara Loughran would never. Chris Hixon would never. Luke Hoyer would never. Martin Duque Anguiano would never.

Peter Wang would never. Alyssa Alhadeff would never. Jamie Guttenberg would never. Meadow Pollack would never."

In one of the most powerful demonstrations of silence ever witnessed, she stopped speaking and stood facing the crowd for several minutes on end, tears streaming down her face. The silence was disrupted at the end by an alarm.

She closed with a gut-wrenching statement: "Since the time that I came out here, it has been six minutes and twenty seconds. The shooter has ceased shooting and will soon abandon his rifle, blend in with the students as they escape and walk free for an hour before arrest.

Fight for your life before it's somebody else's job."

Breaking Down González's Speech

Message Type: Call-Out
Tone: Blunt/fierce/kick-ass/emotionally vulnerable

The core purpose of González's speech was to challenge the status quo on gun ownership regulations. Her powerful use of silence was a demonstration of the time it had actually taken to end her classmates' lives. Creating a lengthy radio silence is usually a huge risk in a live speech but she handled it with such dignity that it worked to her advantage to punctuate her message. In addition, she personalized her speech by creating a connection to her classmates and sharing some of their unique characteristics. This ensured that the audience was thinking of them as individuals rather than numbers. She also employed a powerful use of repetition. By repeating "would never," over and over, without specific descriptors, she left room for the audience to imagine what those children would never be able to do again.

One of the strengths of this speech was mixing power with emotional vulnerability. Previously we have highlighted that a combination of vulnerability and strength is needed for evolutionary leadership. González's speech was a potent mixture of both.

Russell Brand's Speech

Controversial British comedian Russell Brand called out and dismantled the immigration argument in under ninety seconds in one of his stand-up sketches.[ii]

"Not only is Fox News bigoted, it is also misleading. I once watched it for twelve hours and there was not one story about foxes.

Just stories about immigrants really. Not even stories. Just shouting."

Then at the top of his voice, he took on the persona of a journalist on Fox News, yelling, "Immigrants... Immigrants... Immigrants..." before reverting back to his own persona and saying, in a calmer tone while rolling his eyes "Alright!"

He then continued, "You know that an immigrant is just someone who used to be somewhere else," and his audience burst into fits of laughter.

He takes on the Fox News persona again and screams, "Agggggggggghhhhh. Have you always been there?"

He switches to the voice of the immigrant who says, politely, "No, no, no, I used to be over there."

He switches back to the Fox News persona, and screams, running away. "Keep still," he yells, and follows in an exaggerated tone, "I can't relax if people are moving around."

Continuing in a dramatic, exaggerated voice, he adds, "Keep still on the spherical rock in infinite space, with imaginary geopolitical borders that have been drawn in according to the economic reality of the time. Do not pause to reflect that the free movement of global capital will necessitate free movement of a global labor force to meet the demands created by the free movement of that capital. That is a complex economic idea and you won't understand it." He finishes by yelling, "Just keep still on the rock!"

Breaking Down Brand's Speech

Message Type: Call-Out
Tone: Comic, smart, challenging status quo

Brand's speech is genius, because it takes us out of the myopic thinking around borders and reminds us of our existence on a deeper level. It smashes up the immigration argument because it takes us into a more evolutionary perspective of our humanity and out of the polarized view of "us and them."

SPEECHES THAT CALL IN

Reminder: Messages that call in encourage others who have a similar perspective to you to expand their thinking or take action.

Andrew Sullivan's Speech

On a video recording entitled *The Big Think: It Gets Better, But Not Through Politics,* Andrew Sullivan gave his view on how gay rights need to evolve out of the framework of conventional politics.[iii]

"The great struggle for gay people is that politics is just not going to work for us. The idea that these politicians will bring us equality has always been a complete delusion. The only thing that brings us equality is our own testimony and our own lives," he said.

He went on to share that, "Although I believe we do have a politics and what I tried to do in the 90s was to redefine gay politics by getting away from victimhood and the new-left's interpretation of homosexuality to what I think is the truth about it—and our emotional core as human beings."

He highlighted his positive views about sex before saying, "In the end, however much sex you want to have, and with however many people, and in however many ways, to love and be loved is what human beings really want."

He told the audience, "When I first started talking about gay marriage, most people in the gay community looked at me as if I was insane or possibly a fascist reactionary, whereas the next generation of gay men and gay women have internalized and understood that *of course* it's their right to do this. Why would they not? And that has happened in twenty years. That is a profound shift in self-consciousness. And that shift in self-consciousness has affected the consciousness of everybody else. Especially our families."

He asked, "Would my father have ever moved from one position to another were it not for his son telling him the truth?" and answered, "No. I don't think so. And that is our strength."

"What we are going to do is shift consciousness." He highlighted how that consciousness is continuing to shift

"We've gone from 15 percent of support for marriage rights in 1989 to 52 percent today. We have 75 percent support for gays openly serving in the military. We have 80 percent for non-discrimination in employment. And yet we still have politicians that can't do it. And our goal is to simply forget those politicians."

His belief is that, in the end, society "will have to adjust to us because it will seem absurd not to," and that "If you change the society and the culture, the politics will follow."

When he talked about how to change society, he took it back to the grassroots level. "It's one thing seeing a character on a TV show or a celebrity being gay. It's a totally different thing when you know your brother, or your friend, or the dude you hung out at high school with is gay. So I have always believed in a way that if every gay person really did come out, it would be over."

Breaking Down Sullivan's Speech

Message Type: Call-In
Tone: Optimism and hope for more equality in the future, calm, measured

The speech has a powerful social evolutionary context because it shares the vision of the collective power we have to create shifts in consciousness. Grounding this speech in statistics also supports the understanding that society is evolving towards greater acceptance and understanding. It engages hope and optimism in those who were being called in to feel that progress is being made.

Valarie Kaur's Speech

Valarie Kaur began her visionary speech by taking her audience to a moment in history when her grandfather arrived in the US.[iv] "On Christmas Eve 103 years ago, my grandfather waited in a dark and dank cell. He sailed by steamship across the Pacific Ocean from India to America leaving behind colonial rule, but when he landed on American shores, immigration officials saw his dark skin, his tall turban (worn as part of his Sikh faith) and saw him not as a brother, but as a foreign suspect and threw him behind bars where he languished for months."

She went on to relate how a lawyer had helped to set him free.

She then took her listeners on a historical tour of the 1900s, highlighting that "when his Japanese-American neighbors were rounded up and taken to their own detention camps in the deserts of America, he went out to see them when no one else would."

She talked of what led her to the law profession (in the aftermath of 9/11, a man that she called uncle was murdered), and how she became a lawyer like the man who freed her grandfather, because she also wanted to help. She shared how she "joined a generation of activists fighting detentions and deportations, surveillance and special registration, hate crimes and racial profiling" and how she believed her actions were "making the nation safer for the next generation."

She personalized her story further, turning it to her son: "On Christmas Eve, I watched him ceremoniously put the milk and cookies by the fire for Santa Claus, and after he went to sleep I then drank the milk and ate the cookies. I wanted him to wake up and see them gone in the morning—I wanted him to believe in a world that was magical." She spoke of her concerns that she is leaving to her son "a world that is more dangerous than the one that I was given." She talked of her concerns around "raising a brown boy in America. A brown boy that may someday wear a turban as part of his faith."

She then connected her audience to all the challenges that we currently face: "In America today, as we enter an era of enormous rage, as white nationalists hail this as their great awakening, as hate acts against Sikhs and our Muslim brothers and sisters are at an all time high, I know, I know that there will be moments, whether on the streets or in the schoolyard, where my son will be seen as foreign, as suspect, as a terrorist—just as black bodies are still seen as criminal, brown bodies are still seen as illegal, trans bodies are still seen as immoral, as indigenous bodies are still seen as savage, as the bodies of women and girls are still seen as property."

She went on to share her profound and hopeful vision, "As I close my eyes, I see the darkness of my grandfather's cell and I can feel the spirit of ever-rising optimism in the Sikh tradition within him. And so, the mother in me asks: What if, *what if this darkness is not the darkness of the tomb, but the darkness of the womb?* What if our America is not dead, but a country that is waiting to be born, what if the story of America is one long labor, what if our grandfathers and grandmothers are standing behind us now, those who survived occupation and genocide, slavery and [...] political assault. What if they're whispering to us tonight, 'You are brave'? What if this is our national great transition? What does the midwife tell us to do? 'Breathe' and then, 'Push.' Because if we do not push we will die, if we do not push our nation will die. Tonight, we will breathe, and tomorrow, we will labor in love, through love, and your revolutionary love is the magic we will show our children."

Breaking Down Kaur's Speech

Message type: Call-In
Tone: Connecting, optimistic, visionary, strong, powerful

Kaur gives a powerful social evolutionary speech, taking her audience on a profound journey. She grounds her message in the history of her family and the very real challenges of prejudice that exist today. She then takes her audience into her vision, asking the question, "What if this darkness is not the darkness of the tomb, but the darkness of the womb?" Her imagining is powerful because even though she highlights the existing issues, she also allows the audience to conceive that, however difficult the current paradigm, it could be the birth of something, rather than its end. The whole premise of social evolution, and everything that we have shared in this book so far, is built upon the hope, the possibility, the dream, that we are part of a great shift in consciousness, and Kaur eloquently opens the door for this shift to be imagined.

One of the core factors of Kaur's speech was her delivery. She presented in a very strong, crisp manner. Her tone of voice ensured that although she was referencing her grandfather's past, it did not feel sentimental. Her speech had such strength because of the combination of the stories she used and her pinpoint delivery, making it feel like an arrow straight to the heart.

Van Jones's Speech

When Van Jones delivered his hour-long speech *Revolutionary Love: Building a Movement with Love + Power* on April 28, 2017, at Middle Collegiate Church, in New York City, he asked the audience to look at not what they were against, but what they were for.[v]

About a quarter of the way into his speech he stated, "I love Obama. And her husband. Don't leave him out. That's wrong!"

And went on to say, "I love Obama because she said, 'When they go low, we go high.' And when she said it in the convention in 2016, nobody in the room said she was wrong. That she was a sellout. That she was turning the country over to fascists."

He then turned this concept directly towards his audience, creating a connection to those who saw the world in a similar way. "That's who you are. You love everybody. [...] You all love critters. You all love polar bears, and polar bears would eat your butt. You all weird, man. You been crazy your whole life. Hate to see anybody bullied. Hate it. Hated it when you were a kid, in your household, in the school, on the playground. You had cousins who could watch horror movies. You couldn't watch them. Too sensitive. And now you gonna try and out-ugly Donald Trump. You are not going to succeed, I hate to be rude!"

He goes on to describe how he sees the main way we approach the issues we are facing as counterproductive, "The political challenge is very straightforward, but nobody wants to deal with it. On the one hand, you do have one-party minority rule in America. [...] It would be very easy to say 'We have the numbers, they cheated, they suck. [...] He gonna be impeached tomorrow anyway. And we don't have to do anything except be mad and righteous. And wait till 2018 or 2020—then we will have the House and the Senate [...] and then we will show them a thing or two.' Here is the problem. That exact formula is called 2009. You literally just did that, then what did you get?

The Tea Party and Donald Trump. We can do the seesaw all you want to, or we can try and find a third way out. And that is what this Revolutionary Love project, and the Love Army, and your congregations, and your networks are secretly praying for. That there can be a third way out."

Jones defines how he sees being "against" as part of the problem, asking his audience, "Where do we look now for examples? It is easy to move a movement on the front end that is 'anti-something.' In fact my entire life with the progressive left has been defined by having movements that were 'anti-something.' Anti-war, anti-racist, anti-sexist, anti-pollution. We have got so good at defining what we are against that what we are against now defines us. You can't even describe who you are without describing what you are against. That's not freedom. Ask somebody, 'What are you against?' and get some popcorn. You will get to the bottom of the bucket of popcorn before they even take a breath. They will explain to you every oppression in the history of oppression, how it works and functions and how you need to own your privilege, [...] and by the time they get finished, 'Can I just ask you one more question. What are you for?' And you will hear crickets. What are we for? I think we are trying to build something that isn't just a resistance. That is not just another anti-. I think there is a deeper calling, and a deeper prayer, and a deeper hope. I think we are trying to build a pro-democracy movement that can deliver on human rights, that can deliver on sane ecological policy for the children of all species."

He goes on to describe that how we show up has the greatest effect, highlighting this in the example of Mandela. He says that when Mandela finally got out of prison, "He could have been the angriest human born." He describes how a "racist, authoritarian, fascist government were forced to let him go and meet with them." He then sets the scene for how Mandela created change. "He sits down across the table from them. Mandela in Afrikaans told the story of the Afrikaner people and how they had been able to achieve things and do things. He talked about their great generals and agricultural achievements. [...] Everyone in that room knew it was over. Because you're dealing with an opponent who has a higher vision of you than you do. Dignity. Nobility. More than you can imagine for yourself."

He tells the audience, "I'm not calling you out, I am calling you up to your own greatness. I'm not fighting against you, I am fighting for you."

(This is a short section of a one-hour speech. See www.equalityhive. com/book-resources/ for the whole speech.)

Breaking Down Jones's Speech

Message Type: Call-In
Tone: Comic, direct, bridge-building, evolutionary, informal

Jones's speech is social evolutionary on multiple levels and is an outstanding example of using humor and informal dialect to create a connection with the audience and call them in. Firstly, beginning with Michelle Obama's "When they go low, we go high," sets the context for his speech. Secondly, he builds a strong connection to his audience by showing them he understands their sensitivity and who they are, creating a powerful bridge for calling them in to a different way of seeing the world. Thirdly, he turns to the current political climate, and shows how the way that we are attempting to create a different reality—going against, rather than for—is not an effective solution.

He goes on to give a powerful example in Mandela and brings into context the behaviors of one of the most powerful, transformative leaders of our time; he then summarizes why Mandela's actions worked.

His assertion that he is calling the audience to their own greatness is a prime example of social evolutionary leadership and a bridge into another world.

SPEECHES OF SUPPORT

Reminder: Messages of support advocate for a particular group.

Bill de Blasio's Speech

Following some of the changes that surrounded the 2016 election,

New York Mayor Bill de Blasio delivered a direct and powerful social evolutionary speech of support to the people of his city.[vi]

"Here is my promise to you as your mayor. We will use all the tools at our disposal to stand up for our people. If all Muslims are required to register, we will take legal action to block it. If the federal government wants our police officers to tear immigrant families apart, we will refuse to do it. If the federal government tries to deport law-abiding New Yorkers who have no representation, we will step in and build on the work of the city council to provide these New Yorkers with the lawyers they need to protect them and their families."

He continued his message of support by assuring, "If the justice department orders local police to resume stop and frisk, we will not comply. We won't trade in neighborhood policing for racial profiling."

He reassured his constituents that, "If there are threats to federal funding for Planned Parenthood of New York City, we will ensure women receive the healthcare they need. If Jews or Muslims or members of the LGBT community, or any community, are victimized and attacked, we will find their attackers, we will arrest them, we will prosecute them."

He finished by reminding his audience of the strength of their community. "This is New York. Nothing about who we are changed on election day. We are always New York."

Breaking Down de Blasio's Speech

Message type: Support
Tone: Strong, direct, clear, kick-ass

One of the key strengths of Mayor de Blasio's speech is his use of problem to solution. He connected to the very real issues that his constituents were facing, meeting them where they were, before reassuring them that there would be direct actions of support if, and when, those issues arose. He also reinforced the idea of community within the container of New York, so that there was a feeling of inclusivity and belonging in a time when prejudice and hatred were creating an environment of polarization and us-and-them.

Justin Trudeau's Speech

Canadian Prime Minister Justin Trudeau's apology to the LGBTQ+ community for past transgressions of the Canadian government—a speech that he delivered in The House of Commons—was also an iconic message of support.[vii]

"It is with shame and sorrow, and deep regret for the things we have done that I stand here today and say: We were wrong. We apologize. I am sorry. We are sorry."

The formal apology was delivered in the Canadian House of Commons, as Trudeau stated, "Today we finally talk about Canada's role in the systemic oppression, criminalization, and violence against the lesbian, gay, bisexual, transgender, queer, and two-spirit communities. While we may view modern Canada as a forward-thinking progressive nation, we can't forget our past. The state orchestrated a culture of stigma and fear around LGBTQ+ communities and in doing so destroyed people's lives."

He went on to admit, "Our laws bolstered and emboldened those who wanted to attack nonconforming sexual desire. Our laws made private and consensual sex between two same-sex partners a criminal offense leading to the unjust arrest, conviction, and imprisonment of Canadians. Women and men were abused by their superiors and asked demeaning probing questions about their sex lives. Some were sexually assaulted. Those who admitted they were gay were fired, discharged, or intimidated into resignation. They lost dignity, they lost careers, and had their dreams—and indeed their lives—shattered. To those who were left broken by a prejudiced system and to those who took their own lives—we have failed you."

He continued, "It is our collective shame that you were so mistreated. And it is our collective shame that this apology took so long. Many who suffered are no longer alive to hear these words and for that, we are truly sorry."

He ended with a promise of a different outcome for the LGBTQ+ community. "We promise to consult and work with individuals and communities to right these wrongs and begin to rebuild trust. We will ensure that there are systems in place so that these kinds of hateful practices are a thing of the past."

Breaking Down Trudeau's Speech

Message type: Support
Tone: Apologetic, regretful, reconciliatory, peacemaking

Trudeau's was a classic speech of support, including all the hallmarks such as taking responsibility and admitting, on behalf of the people of Canada, the prejudices of the past and how they impacted the LGBTQ+ community as a whole.

This speech also has the potential to unite. When, as a leader, Trudeau takes such a humble position of owning the prejudices of his people as a whole, he also simultaneously opens up the possibility for those who do not share this point of view to question the stand they take. He builds a bridge to a more evolutionary viewpoint on sexual equality.

EXERCISE: CRAFTING A SPEECH

Whether or not you have a speech to give currently, it can be useful to practice crafting a speech and honing your delivery style. There are basically two parts to crafting your speech. What you say and the way you say it. First determine the kind of speech you want to give (call in, call out, disrupt, unite, support, etc.). Then craft a speech that:

- Has an opening line that draws your listeners in
- Takes your audience on an emotional journey
- Connects with their current challenges
- Shares a story
- Gives a vision of a different reality.

Determine the tone of your speech and the mood you want to create.

Although our focus has been content, you will also need to consider delivery. Which words or phrases will you emphasize? Where will you use pause to create effect? Is there anywhere in your speech that repeating a certain word or phrase would give it more emphasis? Will you learn the script or make bullet points? If it is live or recorded, will you deliver it differently?

CHAPTER SUMMARY

- Although we tend to think of many of the great speeches of our modern times as being spontaneous, most of them were carefully crafted in advance.

- Because speech is a right that most of us have, we don't always consider the difference between a speech that comes naturally and one that we have prepared.

- Often we assume that we should automatically know what to say in every circumstance.

- If we are a planner, we end up over-rehearsing our speech, sounding mechanical and void of energy.

- When you are crafting your speeches, you need to consider how to keep them alive.

- With a speech you can disrupt, unite, call in, call out and support.

- Each of your messages is going to have a specific tone, and this extends beyond the sound of your voice into the atmosphere you've created with the words you've spoken.

- Many speeches that are spoken out loud don't have the same power when directly translated into the written word, because they lack the tone of voice that they were conveyed with.

Chapter 9
Writing

In an iconic episode of *Star Trek: Deep Space Nine*, Benjamin Sisko, the captain of the space station, collapses into unconsciousness, and has a full sensory vision of himself as an under-appreciated science fiction magazine writer in 1950s America.[i]

As a black man heading a space station in the twenty-fourth century, in a world where racism has been eradicated, Sisko is catapulted into a twentieth-century reality, and exposed to a world where racism is still prevalent. He writes the story of his future self as the captain of a space station but is unable to get it printed because the white, male-dominated publishing industry at that time was not prepared to envision a future reality where a black man is a leader and a hero.

Although Sisko's tale was ultimately fiction, it holds a powerful metaphor for you as a writer. The Sisko from the 1950s was able to look forward and see a vision of what could be, and articulate it in writing, despite how everything and everyone around him said that the world he could see was not possible. The preacher in the episode told him, "You are both the dreamer and the dream." You have a similar mission with your own writing: To reach beyond the current reality and show a world that can exist regardless of what you see around you. To be both the one that creates and the one that becomes the dream.

In this chapter, our main focus is going to be how you share key elements of your message in writing. We'll look at formal and informal styles so that you can get clearer on how to most effectively represent yourself in the written form. We'll also briefly touch upon the context in which you write, so you can create the most effective environment to express your vision in writing.

FORMAL OR INFORMAL WRITING STYLE

I've lost count of the times I've witnessed it since being in publishing consultancy. A dynamic and brilliant leader with a following of thousands would come to consult with me. They ticked all the boxes in terms of being an influential leader—they had a massive social media presence, tens of thousands read their blog and they were loved and adored by their followers. Yet when it came to securing a conventional publishing deal, they had consistently fallen short. First, I'd ask to see their blog posts—usually well-articulated with a ton of engagement.

Then I'd ask to see their book manuscript, and more often than not, *it would read the same as their blog posts.*

As a general rule, your blog post sounds more like your speaking voice, but if you are writing a non-fiction book—especially if you want a publishing deal—most publishers will be looking for a manuscript that is written more formally. This is because a greater percentage of them are still currently adhering to more conventional writing styles, and an informal tone is not going to cut it.

A formal writing style is one that adheres to the conventions of writing. It is going to be grammatically correct, with carefully structured sentences that are more professionally constructed and sometimes less personal. An informal writing style is more casual. It is not going to conform to strict conventions and will resemble the spoken word for most people (unless you speak very formally).

The other key consideration for whether you choose an informal or formal style is your audience. You need to consider what the best way to communicate with them is so that your message is effectively received.

In the following samples, we'll look at informal and formal writing styles that work well, from several different social evolutionary fields, so that you can get clearer on using the tool of writing most effectively for your purpose.

INFORMAL WRITING STYLES

An informal writing style will deliver a number of benefits:

- If your own speaking style is fairly informal, then an informal writing style will feel and sound more familiar to you
- If your audience is more likely to speak in an informal style, then it can create a more recognizable connection to them
- You can often have more fun with an informal style, using street-smart language and slang
- It can feel a lot more personal.

Dr. Venus Opal Reese

If you are self-publishing, you can have a bit more flexibility with the rules of formality. Dr. Venus Opal Reese used an informal style in her book *The Black Woman Millionaire: A Revolutionary Act that DEFIES Impossible.*[ii] On the back cover she wrote:

Becoming a Black Woman Millionaire is a revolutionary act. It flies in the face of history. It's telling history to kiss your Black A$$.

Look, sis, do I have permission to tell the truth about why you are not a black woman millionaire—yet? Can I just talk to you, sister to sister? No pretense, no political correctness, just real and raw?"

She goes on to say:

I can tell you why your business hasn't bloomed.

Why you stay at a job that is beneath you.

Why no matter how hard you work or how many degrees you get, you live paycheck to paycheck.

I can tell you the real reason you lie awake at night tired, stressed, and sleepless, because no matter how much you slave at your business or at that job or in that cubicle, you never feel like you are enough or that you make enough.

Do you want to know the truth about why you make big moves and big money [...] but you are "cash-flow poor"—regardless of your high net-worth tax bracket?

Then this is the book, the answer, and the salve for hurts you might not even know you're carrying that directly affect your money.

She connects to you as the reader directly. Immediately you are drawn in and want to learn more. You can feel her wisdom—

which comes from her direct experience—and the choice of informal writing makes it feel like she is casual, in your living room, talking to you as a friend who is going to share a secret with you.

Lindsay King-Miller

In *Ask a Queer Chick*, Lindsay King-Miller states the purpose of her book: "It won't tell you foolproof ways to meet hot, available women (although I can tell you that my friend Mickey introduced me to the person I ended up marrying, so maybe hit her up).[iii] Instead, it will talk you through some of the major roadblocks you might face on your journey through the joy and heartache of queerness."

She says her book will offer her reader "…time-tested tips on confidence, communication, self-advocacy, and generally being the best possible version of yourself," and "that when you find the person who makes your heart (and genitals) sing, you can sweep her off her feet."

She also tunes into some of the challenges that her readers face: "Whether you're struggling with discovering who you are, coming out, hookups, breakups, or anything in between," before highlighting the outcome for her readers: "*Ask a Queer Chick* is here to help you get through it with style, wit, and self-love."

In a similar style to Dr. Reese's, you get the feeling that King-Miller is right there with you on the journey. Her use of humor ("although I can tell you that my friend Mickey introduced me to the person I ended up marrying, so maybe hit her up"), alongside acknowledging some of the roadblocks that her reader might face, means she grounds her writing in the challenges that her reader might be looking to overcome while simultaneously lifting the mood to one of ease and optimism by showing them a vision of "style, wit and self-love."

Juno Dawson

On a similar topic, in *This Book is Gay*, Juno Dawson writes in an even more informal style than the one above.[iv] She states:

> In short, we have to be able to laugh at ourselves, whatever our identity, or we're in for a long-haul life. So, yeah, *This Book Is Gay* isn't entirely serious all the way through (although we do deal with some MEGA SAD FACE topics).

> This is something different from the loads of dreary textbooks about gender and sexuality politics that are already out there. This book is serious, but it's also fun and funny.

> The whole point of coming out is that we have the FREEDOM to be who we are. When did that stop being FUN?

If you're new to the club, you're lucky because being L or G or B or T or * is SUPER FUN. You're FREE now and don't have to HIDE.

Dawson's use of capitalization, and humorous colloquial phrasing such as "mega sad face" makes her personality stand out in her writing, creating a highly vibrant and welcoming environment, making her reader feel that she is right there beside them, and encouraging them to relax about coming out.

BRIDGING FORMAL AND INFORMAL STYLES

Some writing bridges the world of formality and informality. The following examples use a mixture of formal and informal approaches in their style.

Roxane Gay

"I embrace the label of bad feminist because I am human. I am messy. I'm not trying to be an example. I am not trying to be perfect. I am not trying to say I have all the answers. I am not trying to say I'm right. I am just trying—trying to support what I believe in, trying to do some good in this world, trying to make some noise with my writing while also being myself."[v]

Gay's writing feels personal, but within a formal context. Although the sentence structure is fairly formal, the repetition of the use of "trying" and "not trying" makes the excerpt very human, raw and real, giving the piece an edge of vulnerability that means it is relatable to the reader's own journey; it creates informality as they switch between what she is—and is not—trying to do as part of the feminist movement.

Layla Saad

In Chapter 3, we highlighted Layla Saad and the journey that she had when her blog post, *I Need to Talk to Spiritual White Women about White Supremacy (Part One)*, was released.[vi] Saad's post bridged both formal and informal writing styles on the subject of white supremacy, following the events that occurred in Charlottesville.

She wrote in her post, "Unless you have been living under a rock for the past few days, you'll know that a white nationalist rally took place in Charlottesville in the US over the weekend. Many were injured. A woman, Heather Heyer, who was known as a passionate advocate for the disenfranchised, was killed. A young black man was surrounded by these hateful neo-Nazis and beaten with poles. Yes, POLES."

Later on she speaks directly to the fear that the pictures from Charlottesville generated: "The images of angry white men rallying with torches is one of the most frightening things I've seen in recent times."

Further on in the post she goes on to describe her childhood in the UK. "One day, when I was about 6 or 7 years old, a new boy started coming to play at the park. And the first time I saw him, he sneered at me and told me that my skin was the colour of poop.

My face still feels red just thinking about it. I felt so ashamed. I couldn't say a thing. All I felt was the shame of being in the skin that I was in. Of not being white like everyone else. I ran straight home with tears in my eyes."

Further on she shares, "As I grew up, I experienced more instances of racial prejudice like this. Some small, some big. Each time, I took these situations and buried them deep inside of myself," and this added to the story that being who she was "was intrinsically wrong and unworthy."

After highlighting some other poignant aspects of her history growing up, she takes the reader to the present day. "Fast forward 18 years later to this weekend and these images..." and as she shows some of the most harrowing pictures from Charlottesville, she writes, "Slavery may not (technically) be legal. But racism flourishes. And so do the oppressive systems of white supremacy that allow white privilege and racial discrimination to still exist."

She then turns the focus on her readers. "Which brings me to you, my dear white sister." She asks, "I'm wondering how you're feeling right now as you are reading this letter. Uncomfortable? Outraged? Helpless? Ashamed? Wanting to do everything you can to stop this and yet feeling like you have no idea what you can do or say?"

"I hear you. It's overwhelming and confusing and triggering as hell.

"But while for you this may be really emotionally distressing, for people of colour this is way more than that. This is about the right to black lives. About black human rights. About the simple right to exist in the skin we were born in without harassment, discrimination or injustice."

She rounds up by speaking about, "The hypocrisy of entrepreneurs who claim that their work is all about empowering others, and yet, when the time comes to speak up about white supremacist Nazis and racial injustice, they are silent."

Saad's article is one that bridges the formal and informal style. She uses a formal style to eloquently confront the issue of white supremacy, while simultaneously using an informal style in her storytelling to create a strong connection to her reader. Mentioning how she felt when she was bullied by that boy, and letting the reader know that it still makes her go red when she thinks of it today, creates a strong emotional connection to Saad and her story.

Her blog is a powerful call-out, but she also simultaneously builds a bridge to her audience to help them dismantle their point of view. She does this by weaving in stories that create a deep connection to her audience and then, when they have felt her pain and they understand her position, she calls her white readers out on their silence.

FORMAL WRITING STYLES

A formal writing style will deliver contrasting benefits to an informal style:

- It can sound more authoritative and professional in some settings
- If your audience is more likely to respond to a formal style, it can be a wiser choice (i.e. if your audience is more conservative in nature)
- It can be a solid container for breaking up stereotypes and smashing up preconceived perceptions, particularly in a social evolutionary context
- For publishers and some magazines, it can be the deal breaker for getting an article or book published.

bell hooks

In *Feminism is for Everybody*, bell hooks expresses her vision of a world of sexual equality.[vii]

She opens her visionary piece by asking the audience to envision a world of equality: "Imagine living in a world where there is no domination, where females and males are not alike or even always equal, but where a vision of mutuality is the ethos shaping our interaction. Imagine living in a world where we can all be who we are, a world of peace and possibility."

She highlights how it is only through collective change—of the entire human race—and working with intersectionality, that we can achieve such a vision, and that the "feminist revolution alone will not create such a world; we need to end racism, class elitism, imperialism."

She goes on to describe how the world will be when her vision is realized: "… It will make it possible for us to be fully self-actualized females and males able to create beloved community, to live together, realizing our dreams of freedom and justice, living the truth that we are all 'created equal'."

She then draws her audience in: "Come closer. See how feminism can touch and change your life and all our lives. Come closer and know firsthand what feminist movement is all about. Come closer and you will see: feminism is for everybody."

This classic visionary speech works well in a formal style. She talks of social evolutionary concepts such as "fully self-actualized females and males," "beloved community," and "living the truth that we are all 'created equal'." Her formal style draws the reader in, and she invites them further to "come closer" to the world that she sees, building a bridge and uniting the reader with her vision of equality.

Akwaeke Emezi

Trans author Akwaeke Emezi received a lot of press for their debut novel *Freshwater.* In an article for *The Cut,* they shared a moment from their journey in a formal style.[viii]

"While my gender had asserted itself in different ways since my childhood, one of its strongest features was always a violent aversion toward reproduction, toward having a body that was marked by its reproductive potential—a uterus to carry children, full breasts to feed them with. My first surgery was an outpatient procedure two years after I moved to Brooklyn, a breast reduction: some fat removed from my chest, some glands, some skin, nothing much. It required a letter from my therapist to prove that I was sane."

Emezi said that the surgeon had told them, "I've never heard of anyone like this," before describing him as "an old white man who had performed many surgeries on trans patients, from breast augmentations to double mastectomies."

The surgeon added, "Male to female, female to male, fine. But this in-between thing?"

Emezi wrote, "I ground my teeth into a smile and handed him my letter, along with printed images of the chest I wanted. It was one that felt right for me, one that wouldn't move much, wouldn't sway with pendulous wrongness or leave me gasping shallow breaths because my ribs were encased in the flattening black of a chest binder every day."

They described the journey to surgery, "I paid his office $10,000 skimmed from my student loans and tried not to be angry at the hoops I had to jump through. If I'd asked for an augmentation, it would've been fine, but wanting smaller breasts in the absence of back pain was considered ridiculous enough to require a therapist's approval."

This strongly formal style acts as a container for Emezi's story. Sometimes a more informal approach is necessary to create a connection in a story of this nature, but Emezi has a way of powerfully holding the reader in a formal style that still takes them on an emotional journey. When they write that they ground their teeth into a smile, that statement holds within it the sense of all the frustration and misperception that they experienced. The fact that even though the doctor had worked with many trans patients, he still seemed to show an insensitivity to Emezi's journey, and the way that they captured their frustration at, once again, being singled out, was powerfully held in the formal writing style.

Dunblane Survivors

Following the Parkland shooting in Florida, the survivors and family of the 1996 Dunblane Primary School shooting in Scotland wrote a letter of support to the Parkland students.[ix]

They began, "On the most poignant day of the year for us, we wanted to reach out and offer our deepest and most heartfelt sympathy to you and your teachers and to all the families and friends of those who died at your school on 14th February."

They supported the Parkland students by highlighting, "We have watched and listened with tremendous admiration as you have spoken out for what you believe should happen now: a significant change of attitude towards the availability of guns in your country."

They went on to share the history of their own experience. "Twenty-two years ago today our own lives were devastated when a gunman walked into Dunblane Primary School in Scotland and shot dead sixteen 5- and 6-year-old children and their teacher and injured many more."

Opening their hearts and creating a personal connection, they wrote, "The children who were killed or badly injured were our daughters and sons, our grandchildren, our sisters and brothers, our nieces and nephews, our cousins. The teacher was our wife, our sister, our mother. Five of us are survivors."

They then described the outcome, following the shooting, giving them hope for their own cause. "The gunman owned his four handguns legally, and we knew it had been too easy for him to arm himself with lethal weapons. Like you we vowed to do something about it. We persuaded British lawmakers not to be swayed by the vested interests of the gun lobby, we asked them to put public safety first and to heed what the majority of the British people wanted. Most politicians listened and acted. Laws were changed, handguns were banned and the level of gun violence in Britain is now one of the lowest in the world. There have been no more school shootings."

They continued with a message of encouragement, "We want you to know that change can happen. It won't be easy, but continue to remind everyone of exactly what happened at your school and of the devastation caused by just one person with one legally-owned gun. Never let anyone forget. There will be attempts to deflect you, to divide you and doubtless to intimidate you, but you've already shown great wisdom and strength. We wish you more of that wisdom and strength for this toughest of tasks, one that will be so important in order to spare more of your fellow Americans from having to suffer the way you have. Wherever you march, whenever you protest, however you campaign for a more sensible approach to gun ownership we will be there with you in spirit."

This letter is a classic, formal message of support that contains some key components. The first is sharing the story of those involved and creating the human connection with those who were lost. The second is sharing the story of how their actions changed the gun law in the UK, giving hope for a different outcome. The third is encouraging those campaigning not to give up or be deterred despite the obstacles that are likely to be faced. It spoke of the wisdom of what might come from those who had been there before, and the hope of a different outcome.

Firoozeh Dumas

Firoozeh Dumas's comic memoirs are a tale of her parents emigrating to the US.[x] She tells her reader, "Now that my parents have lived in America for thirty years, their English has improved somewhat, but not as much as one would hope. It's not entirely their fault; English is a confusing language. When my father paid his friend's daughter the complement of calling her homely, he meant she would be a great housewife. When he complained about horny drivers, he was referring to their tendency to honk. And my parents still don't understand why teenagers want to be cool so they can be hot."

She continues, "I no longer encourage my parents to learn English.

I've given up. Instead, I'm grateful for the wave of immigration that has brought Iranian television, newspapers, and supermarkets to America. Now, when my mother wants to ask the grocer whether he has any more eggplants in the back that are a little darker and more firm, because the ones he has out aren't right for *khoresht baenjun*, she can do so in Persian, all by herself. And for that, I say hallelujah, a word that needs no translation."

Dumas's writing is a classic example of both formal and comic writing together. She balances her comic writing with a formal convention—a difficult skill. She builds a bridge into the world of her parents that would otherwise be lost in translation. She endears her parents to readers who may not have an understanding of Persian culture, while simultaneously creating empathy with readers who have parents from other cultures.

EXERCISE: Experiment with formal and informal writing styles. Try writing the following:
- A blog post in a more informal style
- An excerpt from a book in a more formal style

Remember, writing is less about how you actually communicate, and more about what is going to land with your audience. How does this understanding impact your writing style?

WRITING SOMEONE ELSE'S STORY

Written stories can be a powerful way to raise awareness and show support. In her book *A Hope More Powerful Than the Sea*, Melissa Fleming—Senior Advisor to UN Secretary-General and former Chief Spokesperson for the UN Refugee Agency (UNHCR)—tells the incredible story of Doaa Al Zamel, a Syrian refugee who survived remarkable odds.[xi] Doaa was a teenager from Syria who was forced to leave her home during the refugee crisis. She took a boat to Europe, with her fiancé, Bassem, in the hope of starting a new life, but her boat was deliberately capsized. She was one of only eleven survivors out of 500 people on board: Bassem drowned in front of her. She spent four days adrift at sea with corpses floating around her and saved the lives of two small children. She held on for the children and was finally rescued and given a new life in Sweden. She lives with the feeling that if they had done something differently, Bassem might have survived. But Doaa's story is also one of great hope. She shares, "I keep going for him so that his death will mean something. And I keep going out of hope. The hope that one day I and my people will be able to safely return to Syria, the country that I love."

When interviewed about Doaa's story, Fleming highlighted what motivated her to write her book: "There is a saying: statistics are human beings with the tears dried off. Refugees are often treated as statistics, dehumanizing them and allowing for narratives that promote fear and xenophobia. I am afraid that if we didn't tell individual stories, there would be even less empathy, fewer donations and more closed borders. Stories capture people's imaginations and have the power to educate, create sympathy and encourage action."

She also said that when asked "What keeps you going when your work is all about wars and human tragedy?" she answers: "The privilege to witness, through the resilience of refugees, the triumph of the human spirit over injustice and evil."

Her powerful use of narrative to create a personal connection to one refugee's story helps to humanize the refugee crisis.

EXERCISE: If you are sharing the stories of others as a way of creating connection, what are the human elements of the story that you need to highlight in order to build a bridge?

CONTENT AND CONTEXT OF WRITING

When it comes to writing, there is both the *content* and the *context* to consider. For much of this book we have been focusing on the content, but in truth, the context comes first. The context is the container from which you are writing from. It includes all the conditions of writing: you as the writer, your current mood or state, the environment you are writing in, your optimum times for writing, and whether you have thought about or planned what you want to say before you sit down to write. These are all the cornerstones for writing successfully. Ninety percent of the wheel-spinning that occurs for writers can be cut out if you consider the context first. I have gone into this in much greater detail in my previous book, *Write an Evolutionary Self-Help Book,* but am including a summary here.

- **You as the writer** - This includes your story and your evolution. It's where you are on your current journey as the vehicle for your message, and how this comes across in the written word.

- **Your current mood or state** - Time and again I've shared this advice with writers and it has made a profound difference: If you only have one hour to write, and you feel "off," spend 45 minutes getting yourself in a good place to write—whether that's running, stretching, taking a bath, doing some deep breathing, etc.—and 15 minutes writing. You are likely to produce a much higher quality of work if you do this first than if you wrestle with writing for 60 minutes.

- **The environment you are writing in** - Some writers can only work when they are surrounded by noise and movement. Others can only write in complete silence. If you aren't sure which you are, experiment with different environments until you find what works for you (and it may be different depending on your mood). I personally need complete silence to write and lots of movement around me when I edit.

● **The time you are writing** - Some writers only produce quality content first thing in the morning. Others late at night. Make sure you know when you are most productive (in quality and not just quantity).

● **Thinking and planning** - There are three stages to the writing process. Thinking and planning, writing, and editing. For the great majority of writers, each of these need to be carried out at different times. *Yet most unsuccessful writers try to do all three at once.* Preferably have a plan of what you want to write at least one day before you write. Have the writing session on its own. Edit it at a later time. This way, the creative process is untainted by planning and editing, which use different parts of the brain.

THINKING POINT: What kinds of adjustments do you need to make in order to create the most powerful environment for your writing? Experiment with writing: in different places / at different times / when you have planned your writing / after preparing yourself for writing. Note the difference in what you create.

CHAPTER SUMMARY

● Your blog post is likely to sound more like your speaking voice.

● If you are writing a non-fiction book—especially if you want a publishing deal—most publishers will be looking for a manuscript that is written more formally.

● A formal writing style is one that adheres to the conventions of writing.

● An informal writing style is more casual.

● You need to consider the best way to communicate with your audience—formal or informal—so that your message is effectively received.

● Benefits of informal style:

   ● If your speaking style is informal, it will sound more like you

   ● If your audience is informal in their speaking style, it will feel more familiar

   ● You can use street-smart language and slang

   ● It feels more personal.

● Benefits of formal style:

   ● More authoritative and professional in some settings

   ● Depending on your audience, it might be more appropriate

   ● Breaks up stereotypes and smashes up preconceived perceptions, particularly in a social evolutionary context

- For publishers and some magazines, it can be the deal breaker for getting an article or book published.

- When it comes to writing, there is both the *content* and the *context* to consider.

- The context is the container which you are writing from.

- The context includes all the conditions of writing: you as the writer, your current mood or state, the environment you are writing in, your optimum times for writing, and whether you have thought about or planned what you want to say before you sit down to write.

YOU AS A LEADER

Chapter 10	Your Story	180
Chapter 11	Becoming a Catalyst of Change	198
Chapter 12	You on Your Mission	214

In Part Four of this book we will look at you as an evolutionary leader. We'll begin by exploring one of your most powerful tools to connect to your audience—the story you tell and the way that you tell it. You'll see how the way you tell your story can inspire a paradigm shift in others.

We'll also be looking at a question that has been asked frequently throughout history—"How do we actually inspire others to change?"—and applying this question to the social evolutionary model. We'll be looking at two kinds of influencers: those who are inspiring, but don't actually lead others to any kind of change, and those who are catalysts, causing others to both see and live their lives a different way.

In this final part of the book we'll also be looking at you as a leader and how you can have the most well-crafted message in history, but if you haven't considered how you show up to deliver it, you can fall short of making an impact. We'll be looking closely at your leadership qualities and how you unite your own leadership growth journey with your influence on others. By the end of this section you will likely have made a significant leap in how you show up to share your message with the world.

Chapter 10
Your Story

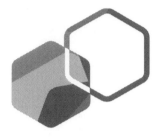

"Stories have the power to create social change and inspire community."

Terry Tempest Williams

How you see your story has a dramatic impact—not only on the way you live your life, but on how you lead your audience.

The way you tell your story can inspire a paradigm shift in others. It can also keep them stuck in their old ways of thinking and being.

As an evolutionary thought leader, one of your most powerful tools is not only the story you tell but the way that you tell it, so that it fires your audience into new possibilities and helps them move beyond any part of their own perception that is limiting them in their way of seeing or being in the world.

YOUR PERCEPTION AND WORLDVIEW

Those who do not have power over the story that dominates their lives, power to retell it, rethink it, deconstruct it, joke about it, and change it as times change, truly are powerless, because they cannot think new thoughts. – **Salman Rushdie**[i]

When it comes to your story, perspective is *everything.*

How you see the world is a mixture of what you were taught and what you experienced. These elements are combined with how you processed those learnings through your own unique character, and how you interpreted these events differently over time. Breaking these parts down further, we can begin to see the many elements that constructed your perception of reality:

- **Your conditioning** - This is everything you were taught, including:
  - Social conditioning - the mainstream views of the society that you were raised in
  - Cultural conditioning - the views of the culture you were raised in
  - Family conditioning - the views of the family you were raised in
  - Personal conditioning - the experiences that you had in your life that caused you to see the world the way you do.

• **Your unique character** - This is how you processed and responded to your conditioning. You may have gone completely with what you were taught, or on the other end of the spectrum, totally rebelled against it. An example of this would be two siblings in a family, where one takes on all the values of the parents, while the other is a renegade. Alternatively, your response may have been more subtle, where you rejected some of what you learned, and took other parts on board.

• **Your evolution** - This is how your perception changes and evolves over time. When you either have a new experience or hear an opposing perspective from someone you feel a strong connection with, your point of view can change or evolve so that you see your story through different eyes.

Unless we have strong mentors who challenge us to see the world from points of view that oppose our own, we can get stuck in myopia, where our social, cultural, family or personal conditioning limits our way of seeing the world. This is especially true if we are surrounded by others who see the world like us. It can be challenging to see our own blind spots, and our view of the world can often be misidentified as the only way, particularly as perception usually *feels* like truth. The neurons in our brains fire and wire together in such a way that they trigger emotional responses that make us feel like our beliefs are undeniably true.

That means your role as an evolutionary thought leader is twofold. Your first charge is to look within to uncover your own conditioning and to recognize the parts of your story that you have taken on as the truth—and which can be challenged to create space for a more expansive view. When you have undertaken the task of deconstructing your own journey, what you have learned, and what you have held true without question, then, and only then, can you begin to deconstruct the stories of those you are leading.

If your audience has similar points of view to yours, then the deconstruction of your own story, and how you share the evolution of your worldview, will likely have a dramatic impact on them. If you are working to challenge the points of view of those who see the world differently from you, then deconstructing your own limitations will enable you to relate more effectively to how their own myopia has been formed.

> ## EXERCISE: THE ELEMENTS THAT CONSTRUCT YOUR STORY
>
> 1. What impact does social conditioning have on your story? Which elements have you taken on board as the truth because of the society you were raised in?
> 2. What impact does cultural conditioning have on your story? Which elements have you taken on board as

the truth because of the culture you were raised in?

3. What impact does family conditioning have on your story? How much of your family's point of view have you taken on as your own?

4. What part does personal conditioning play in your story? Which life experiences have shaped how you see the world?

5. What are your unique characteristics that have caused you to challenge certain aspects of your conditioning? What are your first memories of challenging what you learned?

6. How has your point of view evolved over time? Which perspectives changed with your personal evolution?

The Traumatic Elements of Your Story

It's crucial to understand that the deconstruction of your story is not a mechanical process and can bring with it much turmoil and distress. Particularly when it comes to your personal conditioning, and the things you learned through your life experiences, the past can leave an imprint that can be challenging to come to terms with.

For a number of years I was an expert in the field of emotional trauma. I co-authored a book that was released worldwide in twelve languages by a leading publisher, and I taught all over the world on the subject of how our past experiences influence our point of view.

What I came to understand is that if we experience a traumatic event, it can become imprinted on our subconscious. A similar event, or something that reminds us of what we experienced, can trigger the same biochemical responses as the ones we had at the time of the event. We can be triggered by a smell, a taste, a sound, something we see, or something we touch. If the experience (or series of events) that we went through was severe, it can mean we get triggered into a fight, flight or freeze response on multiple occasions, and this can severely impact our perception and our responses. The work I carried out was one way to process this. I used a technique to reimprint the triggers of the event so it does not create the same automated responses in the body. The recipient is no longer triggered by the sounds, smells, visuals, etc. that remind them of what happened, and the triggers themselves are changed—or reimprinted. Once this has been done, the perception of what happened often changes too.

Unless we find a way to process the information that is held on a subconscious level relating to traumatic events that we experienced in the past, we can find ourselves reliving those events over and over again. This is particularly relevant to many of the issues that social evolutionary leaders work with. If you are striving for racial, social, gender, sexual, religious, refugee equality (and so on), it is likely that either you yourself, or members of your audience, have experienced traumatic events that relate to the lack of equality that you are working to overcome. How you integrate these parts of your story, and how you help others to navigate theirs (including knowing when to bring in outside help), will be crucial in enabling your and others to create a different story. When we are trapped in fear and being triggered over and over again by an extreme experience, it is not usually possible to break out of our story into a new way of seeing things. Because the triggers are so strong, they keep us reliving the event until they are resolved.

THINKING POINT: Are there any elements of your story that have been traumatic (particularly experiences that have included physical or emotional abuse)? What have you done, so far, to process these elements? Is there any further work that needs to be done to integrate these parts?

TELLING YOUR STORY

"Your story needs to speak to your audience's hearts, interests, and worldview."

Michael Margolis [ii]

Your story is one of your most powerful commodities as a catalyst, and the way you tell it can make or break your message.

If you think about the story of your life, there are countless different ways you could share it, and each would have a contrasting effect on your audience. As a female business owner and author who has come from a background of socio-economic challenges, I was once invited to tell my story to a group of young women who were hoping to break out of their own limiting circumstances.

I could have shared my experience growing up in a cut-off town in the North of England where alcoholism, drugs, poverty and violence were rife. I could have shared the pain of growing up feeling disconnected from those around me, with no sense of hope for change. Perhaps it would have had some cathartic value, but it wouldn't have inspired the women to move forward. Instead I shared, "When I was growing up in a factory town in the North of England, much of the career advice that I was given was focused around whether I would work in a shop or a factory. I used to pray that it was going to be a shop. But I had one teacher who helped me see I could be more than I had imagined. He told me I could attend university. And despite my father's response (*Girls don't go to university*), I used my teacher's words as a catalyst to create a different world for myself, eventually building my own company and emigrating to New York." I offered a model of possibility for breaking the poverty cycle.

The same applies to any story in a social evolutionary context. Whatever aspect of equality you are working towards, your own story, and how you tell it, can be a catalyst for your audience. In *The Story Factor,* Annette Simmons highlights, "People don't want more information. They are up to their eyeballs in information. They want faith—faith in you, your goals, your success, in the story you tell. It is faith that moves mountains, not facts. Facts do not give birth to faith. Faith needs a story to sustain it—a meaningful story that inspires belief in you and renews hope that your ideas indeed offer what you promise."[iii] The way that you tell your story is therefore integral to inspiring the faith of those who follow you.

Another key factor for telling your story is that you only need to tell relevant parts to your audience, and not the whole thing! When authors are telling their story in written form, they often treat it as an "information dump" for everything that went before. There are some key elements to storytelling that you will need to apply to be effective. These include:

- **Your lowest moments**: How you felt at your "rock bottom" in relation to the story you are sharing. This needs to be a relevant rock bottom. So, for example, if you are a thought leader in the women's movement who broke out of a violent relationship, you would share a moment when you were most oppressed and what your emotions and thoughts were at that time.
- **Your turning point:** This is the realization that you had that made you change your perspective and take different

actions. For example, if you are a leader in the racial equality movement who had been subjugated in the workplace, this would be the point where you decided you weren't willing to compromise anymore. You would describe how your thought process changed and how you acted differently because of your new perspective. This includes recognizing the old thought processes that were holding you in your old world and the steps that you took to build a bridge into your new world.

● **Your biggest lessons:** What did you learn as a result of this experience and how is that impacting your life today? For example, if you are a transgender woman who faced opposition from her family or community, you would share what you learned from standing strong in your own truth, and how those learnings currently impact your life.

● **Your emotions:** At each stage of your storytelling, you need to engage your audience in the emotional elements of your story. An effective storyteller will take their audience through a full range of emotions, from touching in on how they felt in their lowest moments, to how they moved into faith, hope, and so on. Sharing your emotional journey is the heart of your story and how you connect to the emotions of your audience.

WRITING YOUR STORY

Written well, your story can inspire the reader and create a great connection with you from the outset. But there are several key things to avoid when you write. If you write your life story, do not make it an information dump on what you have been through, just sharing the pain, because you risk sinking your reader emotionally rather than elevating them. In such a case, the story can make the reader feel like you are dwelling on the problem rather than giving them a creative solution.

The following is an example of sharing the pain. This is what *not* to do:

(Notice how you feel when you read this.) "I was born in the north of England. It was an industrial town where most of the employment comes from factories. It was difficult growing up. My father was an alcoholic and for much of my childhood he was in and out of psychiatric hospitals. By the time I was fourteen I was drinking heavily myself, partly to numb the pain of family life, and partly because I had the early onset of bipolar affective disorder, and drinking helped to mask my symptoms."

Instead, find a way to connect to your audience's world:

"From as early as I can remember, I had the feeling that I was seeing the world through different eyes. I recall the first time my father asked me to go get his slippers and remarked that I would make a 'good wife.' I remember feeling a mixture of pride, coupled with a deep and all-pervading feeling that I hadn't simply come here to play the role of wife, and that I could be so much more than this preconceived destiny.

I was three years old at the time."

EXERCISE: WRITING YOUR STORY

Practice writing your story down in different ways.
1. Try it as an information dump where you just share a list of facts about your life.
2. Tel it in a way that shares the pain but doesn't show a different version of reality.
3. Practice telling it in a way that shows your lowest moments and then your greatest realizations and learnings. Ensure that you describe your emotions at each stage. Define and refine this version of your story, and consider how you might adapt it for different audiences.

Your Story Changes as You Evolve

The other crucial factor about telling your story is that in each phase of your evolution, your story changes as you grow. At the beginning of this chapter we talked about perception and how it influences your worldview. As your perception changes, your story does too.

If you have ever had any kind of addictive or destructive behavior that you eventually overcame, the story that you would tell when you were gripped by your habit is different from the one you would tell with all the knowledge and insight you gained from breaking it. Similarly, if you ever had any experience where you were oppressed by another human being or group, and you were able to break out of that oppression, the story you would tell during the period of 'captivity' would likely be different from the one you would tell now. It's crucial to step back and ask yourself where you are on your own journey before you tell your story to others. Being aware of the trajectory of the story you are telling, and knowing where you are within that trajectory, is vital to the tone of the story and how you share it with others.

> **THINKING POINT:** Consider the evolution of one of your stories. How did you see it before you had a particular growth or turning point? What were you thinking and feeling before? How did your perception change at a later point? What thoughts and feelings changed as your perception evolved?

Uncovering Your Biases

Part of our growth as a catalyst is being willing to continuously evolve our perspective and challenge our own point of view, so that we can enable our audience to do the same. Uncovering our biases is one way that we can challenge and change our story.

An example of this is something that happened to me recently. I was handing a dollar bill to a homeless person when something suddenly clicked. It wasn't just that this guy had a dog—a black and white pitbull who reminded me of Bullet, my dog from childhood—it was then that I immediately realized an unconscious bias. I counted back over the last ten times I had done something to help out a homeless person, and seven out of the ten had been someone with a dog. I realized I was being emotionally triggered into a biased behavior, based on my love of animals. My actions weren't inclusive. With the tens of thousands of homeless people living in New York City, the choice of who I gave my money to wasn't fair and equal. It was biased by my history, my experience, and my filters.

A vital aspect of your evolutionary leadership is owning and working with your own biases, because if you are asking others to face and address their own biases and prejudices, you have the best chance of influencing them if you are able to face your own and transform them. Not only does it make you more relatable to your audience, but it also means that the work you are doing is more authentic.

There are two levels to this work. The first is working through any biases you have in your own field of passion. The second is looking at all your unconscious biases in other areas of social evolution. Increasing your awareness and support of more intersectional movements will help to gain momentum for social evolution as a whole and allow more people with a variety of identities to work together effectively.

Starting with your core message, are there any subtle or underlying prejudices that keep you from deeply experiencing equality on all levels? Are there any biases that you haven't faced that, if you brought them out into the open, admitting them (to yourself or others), would make you a more solid leader?

Then move into other areas that aren't your core focus. Consider equality in areas such as:

- Socio-economic issues - poverty, education, health
- Gender
- Sexual identity
- Religion
- Race
- Refugee crisis

See if you can uncover any unconscious biases in these areas.

If you commit to this exercise, you will be spending some time (at least several weeks initially, but maybe several months or more) focusing primarily on your own biases, including your reactions to social media, the news, articles you read, other people's comments, etc. You'll need to examine your thoughts, your emotional triggers and your reactive responses. Also check your tendency to reach out to others who share a similar point of view to yours so that you can reinforce your biases with them, and so that they keep getting normalized. Basically, you'll be overturning everything you think, feel, say and do.

Approaching this exercise with curiosity will give you a different result than if you approach it with the sense that you already know where your biases lie or believe you don't have them. It's also essential to know that you are uncovering biases to further your own contribution to evolving the field you are in, and that you not see them as a weakness or flaw—because uncovering them enables you to become a more intersectional leader.

Once you are aware of your biases, two things can happen. Your awareness can give you greater understanding and empathy, helping you see things more clearly, and your behavior can directly change as a result. For example, I'm still going to help out homeless people with dogs, but I'm also going to be aware of my tendency to react from my emotional triggers and ensure that I am equally inclusive towards those who don't have dogs.

CHAPTER SUMMARY

● As an evolutionary thought leader, one of your most powerful tools is not only the story you tell but the way that you tell it.

● The way you tell your story can inspire a paradigm shift in others. It can also keep them stuck in their old ways of thinking and being.

● When it comes to your story, perspective is *everything.*

● How you see the world is a mixture of what you were taught and what you experienced.

● Elements that construct your reality: Your conditioning (social + cultural + family + personal) / your unique character / your evolution.

● If you had a traumatic experience, it can become imprinted on your subconscious and form a significant part of your story.

● Unless we find a way to process the information that is held on a subconscious level relating to traumatic events that we experienced in the past, we can find ourselves reliving those events over and over again.

● If you think about the story of your life, there are countless different ways you could share it, and each would have a different effect on your audience.

● You only need to tell relevant parts of your story to your audience.

● Tell a combination of your lowest moments / turning

point / biggest learnings / emotions.

● Your story will change with your evolution.

● Uncovering your biases can help you become a more intersectional leader.

Chapter 11
Becoming a Catalyst of Change

How do we actually inspire someone to change? It's the question that influencers have been asking throughout history.

There are fundamentally two kinds of influencers: those who are inspiring, but don't actually lead us to any kind of change, and those who are catalysts, causing us to both see and live our lives a different way.

There is also the consideration of how you adapt your leadership style to reach those you are attempting to influence. If you are dynamic in your approach, then in each new communication you will need to find the 'hook' into the world of your audience so that your message can lead the receiver to think and act in a different way.

In this chapter, we'll be looking at the dynamics of you as the catalyst and how you can adapt to inspire change in a range of different situations.

Inspirers

You've heard them speak in all walks of life. They open their mouths and the room stands still. A sea of faces stares intently, hanging on their every word, the air, thick with their message.

Inspirers hold a powerful potency for their audience. We feel what they say deep within our bones. When we listen to them, read their books and watch their videos, we share a collective experience. Something switches on inside us. It's like we are hearing from an undiscovered part of ourselves through their voice. They speak what we have felt but never shaped into thoughts; they bring the sketches in our minds to life and make them real. Most of us have had this experience at least once, probably even many times in our lives: set on fire by the words of another. If you have, then it's likely that you have also experienced the typical reaction it creates: you go back to your normal life. You may have seen the world through their eyes, but you weren't able to integrate what they shared with you.

Inspirers play a vital role in showing us a vision of reality outside the one we are currently experiencing, but if they are not able to simultaneously demonstrate how to reach that vision, they can fall short of actually influencing us to create change. This often leads to a spiral of dependency, where we go to an inspirer for a 'fix' in the same way we might go to a drug dealer. We attend their keynotes, read their books, watch their videos, take their courses, and each time—though we are being impacted by their words and we feel like we have absolutely got it—we go back to our life and *our thoughts, behaviors, actions and interactions remain exactly the same as before.* We are caught in a spiral of receiving, a passive consumer of inspiration with no direct application.

So, although inspiration can play a vital role in impacting our view of a possible different future, on its own, if it doesn't cause us to follow through in our lives, it is not enough.

Catalysts

Catalysts are practical in their outlook and approach. They influence their audience to *actually create change.* The difference between encountering an inspirer and a catalyst is that while the former doesn't always deeply impact your life, the latter is much more likely to influence a change in your perception, behavior, attitude or actions. Catalysts show you that change is possible and fire you into action.

Catalysts are also inspiring leaders and the ability to spark others is an essential quality of influence, but the difference is that for catalysts, *this is not their only or main quality.* They back their inspiration up with practical solutions that impact the way we show up in the world.

If you want your audience to be more than passive consumers of your message, if you want to support them to go out in the world and see things differently, behave in new ways, challenge or break down existing structures, then it's vital to think about how you and your message combine to create a catalytic effect on your audience.

You don't need to have a specific technique, tool, or method to be a catalyst. Over the last couple of decades there has been a massive trend towards 'how-to self-help' books that give the reader a seven-step program on how to create change in their life. In my early years as a ghostwriter I took on a large volume of these projects, and as time went on I started to question how much some of these methods were actually impacting the reader. It's much easier to market and sell a system that suggests "If you jump through these seven hoops in the correct order you are going to achieve a particular outcome," than it is to convince your audience to dynamically apply your teachings on a multidimensional level across all elements of their lives. This is difficult, largely because we have become consumers of information, eager to invest in books and programs, keen to gather information, but not so willing to actually apply it to our lives. Over time I came to notice the mechanical nature of many of the tools and techniques available and how they didn't necessarily influence the audience to address a different way of being.

A catalyst has some very specific qualities that aren't always as easy to market as a 'seven-step' technique. They tend to respond to each situation uniquely, carefully listening to the individual needs of their audience members, seeking out their blind spots, and illuminating them—shifting their audience into a new perspective and deeply impacting their reality. Suddenly the one being influenced finds themselves beyond the limitations of their experience: their old world crumbles and they are set free. They speak, act or perceive differently. This kind of dynamic leadership can be way more challenging to define, write about, market, and put into a box, yet these qualities make the most profound catalytic leaders.

A New Paradigm of Authentic Catalysts

One of the measures of catalytic leadership can be found in the authenticity of the messenger. As highlighted previously, if you have an interesting concept that looks good on paper but isn't lived out in your life, your sphere of influence will be dramatically different than if what you share is authentically lived out in your life.

For an evolutionary thought leader, this means being impeccable across the board. If you are sharing a message of equality in a particular field, it means examining if you have any blind spots or prejudices in other fields too (see previous chapter for an exercise on this topic). Who you are behind closed doors and how you reconcile that with your public persona is one of the most vital elements of social evolutionary leadership. Is what you teach lived out by you in every moment of your life, on and off screen, or is it a well-rehearsed performance that you pack away at the end of the day? If you can ask yourself this question, not just once but in every moment, and if you can use it to own your authenticity, as a leader, you will enter an entirely different dimension where you are challenging yourself to be real in every word and action.

CHECK-IN: As a social evolutionary thought leader, consider your leadership paradigm. Has there been a tendency towards being an inspirer or a catalyst? What catalytic qualities do you need to develop further?

Think of some of the leaders that have impacted your life. Have there been any true catalysts for you? What were the specific elements of their teaching (their ideas, messages, tone, practical exercises, tools, techniques, processes, leading by example, consistency, strength, vulnerability, etc.) that touched your life? How did you change as a result of what they shared?

CONSIDERING HOW WE CHANGE

What actually causes a person to change? We've touched upon the kind of leader that makes the greatest difference, but there is another level of influencing to consider. That is the person or group that you are aiming to impact. If you are hoping to change someone's perspective or behavior with your message, you have to consider the different ways that behaviors actually change so that you can become dynamic in your approach.

There are some key factors of human behavior that we need to consider before we think about influencing others, including the ways in which others change. Changes can either be explosive or incremental. Explosive changes are the ones that involve a significant transformation in attitude and behavior. They often require a significant shift in lifestyle or approach. The incremental changes are the smaller, often more imperceptible changes that occur over time. They don't usually come with the same fanfare as explosive changes, and they are not always as noticeable from the outside.

THINKING POINT: Determine the different ways you have changed in your life so far.

If you have experienced any dramatic life changes (overcoming addiction, losing a significant amount of weight, breaking out of socio-economic limitations, transforming debt or huge financial challenges, leaving an abusive relationship, overcoming a severe or supposedly incurable illness, etc.), what were the choice points, decisions, perspective changes and behavioral adjustments that led to your transformation?

What about the subtler changes that you have implemented in your life over a longer period? Maybe you have adopted an attitude to health or fitness, unpicked and dealt with your family history, improved your social or financial status, etc. These changes may not have had the same kind of immediate or obvious outcome than the more major ones, but they still required developing a different thought pattern or behavior for you to implement them.

DESIRE TO CHANGE

As you look at those different changes you have made in your life, you will likely notice a common factor in all your successful changes. You actually wanted to see, think, feel or behave differently and you took consistent direct action based on that desire. Yet the elephant in the room that doesn't always get talked about in social evolutionary work is that often the people who we are trying to influence *have no desire to see the world differently.*

One of the most relevant understandings for us as evolutionary thought leaders is to thoroughly grasp that people only change when they actually want to. When we understand this, then our job can be focused more on helping others to shift their mindset in a way that encourages them to see the world differently, than on forcing our belief system on them. This means our task is not to share our point of view or convince people that we are right. Instead it is *to influence others to want to change their point of view.* Our question in every situation, over and over again, consistently and dynamically needs to be "How?" "How can I persuade the person, or group, to want to change the way they see this particular issue? What's in it for them to see the world differently and why should they want to in the first place?" You need to be consistently willing to ask these kinds of questions, over and over again, in different ways and with different groups because without addressing the motivation of the audience you are attempting to reach, you will not be able to tune in to what actually drives their shift in consciousness.

THE "RIGHT" TO INFLUENCE OTHERS

It is also worth noting that the thought of trying to influence the behavior of another can bring up some challenges for us. If you think of all the manipulation we face on a daily basis through advertising, news and social media, or of any personal manipulation you may have experienced in relationships with others, the thought of attempting to influence someone else's point of view might trigger some discomfort. There are two key elements to consider here. The first consideration is that influence and manipulation have distinctly different qualities. While manipulation is an attempt to force your way of seeing things on another so that they might behave in a way that you desire, influence is being a clear channel for your message in such a way that it sparks a change in someone else without you trying to force them. The second consideration is that in a social evolutionary context, we are often influencing others to break down their prejudices and misperceptions so that we can work towards equality for all. We need to ensure our intentions are on influencing, rather than manipulating or forcing, so we can stand strong in our integrity as catalysts for change.

FINDING THE HOOK

That leads us to one of the most powerful tools for influencing others. Finding "the hook."

When I was training to be a drama teacher, I learned about the hook. It was probably one the most important secrets that carried me through my teaching career in socially challenged high schools, as well as working in a specialized unit with teenagers who had severe emotional and behavioral difficulties. When people asked how I had the confidence as a five-foot-three woman, weighing in at not much over one hundred pounds, and with a youthful face, to work with some of the most troubled young people in my city, I would tell them about the hook. When a teacher was struggling to connect with their students, they would come to me for advice, and again, I would teach them about the hook. I still use the hook successfully in my work today.

The hook is the ability to find a bridge into someone else's world. It is the most simple and obvious, yet most overlooked tool for creating a human connection. Instead of imposing your own world on someone else's, you find the fire at the center of their world, and you meet them there.

The hook is not a manipulation tool or a way of faking who you are in order to get a result. Instead, it is a way of showing someone a courtesy by entering their world. It's like saying, "I don't know what our shared interests are, and in the absence of knowing, I'm going to meet you where you are." At the same time the hook needs to have no attachment to an outcome. It isn't "I've done this for you, so now you will do this for me." Instead, it is "I'm opening a door to a connection between us—let's see where that goes."

THINKING POINT: Reflect upon the difference between a skillful use of the hook and manipulation. What's the difference between someone who is clearly playing you to get what they want, versus someone who takes a genuine interest in knowing about you, without pushing their own agenda to the forefront?

I learned the hook from Professor Brian Watkins when I was studying to be a drama teacher at the University of Central England. Professor Watkins was in his seventies, a well spoken English gentleman who had spent much of his life working in some of the most socially deprived areas of the UK. Usually a man of his class and stature would not have been welcomed easily into the socially challenged families and settings that he entered, but he shared with us the secret of how he had always unerringly found the way in with the young people he served.

"I'd always find the entry point," he told us. "And then I would study it endlessly. If a young person liked ferrets, I'd learn all about ferrets. I'd find out what they ate, what their mating habits were, when they slept and how they behaved. I'd learn the lingo, then I'd go to the young person's house. I would only talk about ferrets on the first few visits. I'd go with a long list of questions and I'd listen and let them talk. I'd help them to see that I was willing to enter their world. *Then* when the connection had been made, we could talk business. But only if and when they were ready and that was usually several visits down the line."

Professor Watkins had countless stories about embedding himself in the culture of the young people he supported. He'd go to football matches with them, but not before learning the name of every player on the team, what their history was, and who their rivals were (sometimes finding himself close to some harrowing scrapes in the world of British soccer, which is rife with weapons and hooliganism). He'd go to local community meetings, but not before learning what the challenges were, who the allies were, and the history of the community. Where had they had their funding cut? Who had it affected? He'd learn the names and nicknames of everyone surrounding the young people he supported, often staying up late at night to ensure that every syllable was remembered and pronounced correctly.

I embraced the hook skillfully in my own teaching career—so much so that after just one year of teaching in high school, I was given a special assignment outside of mainstream education to work with severely emotionally challenged young people. It was a significant jump in my pay rate and a position usually only given to senior teachers who had been teaching for decades.

One of my roles was to help young people who were refusing to go to school, to return to the classroom. On one occasion I met with a young man, David, who hid inside a locked wardrobe every time a school official visited. For several months, nobody had been able to coax him out. On my first visit to his home, while he was shut inside his wardrobe, I looked around his room and found two WWE wrestling figures. I went home that night and learned the names and all the moves. It didn't matter that I was a peace activist and that wrestling wasn't my thing. What mattered was the hook into David's world.

When I returned the next day, David hid in his wardrobe. I picked up the two wrestling figures of John Cena and The Rock. "Who do you think does the best People's Elbow?" I asked. Immediately I saw his eyes appear at the slats of the wood in the wardrobe. "Some people say it's Cena, but I think it's The Rock," I told him casually. The door of the wardrobe flew open. "It's definitely The Rock," he told me, his eyes alight. I visited three times on consecutive days and we talked only about wrestling. On the fourth day we made a deal: I'd do some math work with him and at the end we'd talk wrestling. After five days we talked about why he was refusing to go to school and what he needed to have in place to get back to school (which was actually something very simple and solvable). Within ten days he was back in the classroom.

In Chapter 3, when we considered Daryl Davis's work in supporting members of the KKK to leave the Klan, he highlighted that his method was to talk to them and find the connection. He is basically describing the hook. If you have a message of social evolutionary change, then finding a hook means creating a connection to your audience. This is particularly vital if you are connecting with an audience whose opinion you wish to challenge.

> **QUESTION:** Considering my audience, and the impact that I want to create with my message, what is the most important hook into their world?
>
> This is not a one-time question. It is one that needs to be addressed and considered every time you create a new message, share a post or contribute to the deconstruction of a pattern. What is the most effective bridge that connects your world into theirs?

CHAPTER SUMMARY

● How we inspire someone to change is the question that influencers from all walks of life have been asking throughout history.

● There are two kinds of influencers: those who are inspiring, but don't actually lead us to any kind of change, and those who are catalysts, causing us to both see and live our lives a different way.

● Inspirers play a vital role in showing us a vision of reality outside the one we are currently experiencing, but if they are not able to simultaneously demonstrate how to reach that vision, they can often fall short of actually influencing us to create change. If we go back to our life and *our thoughts, behaviors, actions and interactions remain exactly the same as before,* then we can get caught in a spiral of dependency with an inspiring leader.

● Catalysts are much more likely to influence a change in our perception, behavior, attitude or actions. They show us that change is possible, and they fire us into action.

● One of the measures of catalytic leadership can be found in the authenticity of the messenger.

● Changes can either be (i) explosive—involving a significant transformation in attitude and behavior or (ii) incremental—involving smaller, often more imperceptible changes that occur over time.

● One of the most relevant understandings for us as evolutionary thought leaders is to thoroughly grasp that people only change when they actually want to.

● Questions to ask: "How can I persuade the person, or group, to want to change the way they see this particular issue? What's in it for them to see the world like me and why should they want to in the first place?"

● The hook is the ability to find a bridge into someone else's world. Instead of imposing your own world on someone else's, you find out what the fire at the center of their world is, and you meet them there.

Chapter 12
You on Your Mission

You can have the most well-crafted message in history, but if you haven't considered how you show up to deliver it, you can fall short of making an impact.

For much of this book we have focused on your message, but as we turn to you, the messenger, we need to consider the kind of influence you have over others. There are many components, such as the fire and energy that you have to deliver your message, your own experiences and how they impact the way you see the world, the tools or practices that you use to support yourself, and how these combine to form your presence as a catalytic leader.

There are three, core, interrelated pieces to you as the messenger and each affects the other. Firstly, there is the physical energy you have to carry out your mission. Secondly, there is your mindset for your mission. Thirdly, there is how you show up in the world as a leader and treat those around you. Each of these pieces are essential, and a challenge in one area can have an influence on the others.

(i) ENERGY

Your energy is your capacity to consistently show up and make a difference with what you do. However powerful your message is, your own vitality—the energy you have within you—is what will actually see your mission through. You need to master your own physicality so that you are able to show up with the tenacity needed to make an impact with your words and actions. This includes knowing your physical strengths and how to navigate and support any physical challenges that you may have.

When it comes to your energy, you can either generate it, stagnate it or deplete it:

- **Generate it** - When you generate your energy, you have the tools and practices that support you in your mission. You eat, sleep, exercise, work and spend your time in a way that feeds what you do.
- **Stagnate it** - When you stagnate your energy, you do things mechanically in life that don't drain your energy, but don't feed it either. They are the things that might not be necessary or purposeful anymore, but you do them on autopilot because it's the way it has been for so long.

- **Deplete it** - When you deplete your energy, you do things that zap you, taking your life force from yourself so that you are left tired or drained.

As an evolutionary thought leader, your commitment to your message will include your willingness to look at these aspects within yourself so your main focus is on what generates your energy, with an awareness on what stagnates or depletes it.

THINKING POINT: What generates / stagnates / depletes your energy? What practical actions do you need to take to ensure that the majority of what you do generates the energy you need for your mission? (This is likely to be an ongoing question rather than a one-time inquiry.)

(ii) MINDSET

Your mindset is your ability to mentally stay on track, whatever is happening around you. It includes the ability to cultivate a mindset that supports an optimistic view of the future, as well as knowing—and being able to dismantle—any destructive thought patterns that lead you into catastrophic thinking.

Your mindset includes a combination of your vision, your ability to navigate mental triggers, and cultivating consciousness.

● **Vision** - Within all of us there is the ability to see and create a reality that is different from the one that is playing out around us. Being able to stay connected to your vision, despite any personal, social or global issues that conflict with it, is a core part of evolutionary leadership.

● **Navigating Mental Triggers** - This is how you face your own fears and the doubts of those around you, know when you have been derailed, and learn to refocus, over and over again, whatever the circumstances. It includes any tools or practices you have for both cultivating a strong mindset and knowing when you have been thrown off course.

There will likely be doubters, there may even be haters, but how you navigate your mental response to what occurs is the key to cultivating the mindset for the mission.

● **Cultivating Consciousness** - For much of Chapter 10 on your story, we focused on all the things that you have learned in this lifetime from your experiences and what others have taught you. Your consciousness is the part of yourself that exists outside of everything you have been taught.

If you have any kind of meditation or mindfulness practice, or even if you have ever closed your eyes for a minute and sat in silence, you may be familiar with the part of yourself that exists beyond the noise and static of everything in the world. Your consciousness is also the part of you that knows equality to be our highest human goal. It holds all members of humanity to be equal beyond race, gender, sexual orientation, religion, social standing, wealth, and health and all other identities.

Your consciousness is the part of you that can tune into the possibility of a different version of reality to the one that is playing out and hold faith in the possibility that things can change. It is from consciousness that you connect to your wisdom.

The reason that meditation practices are increasingly popular is because they help us cultivate a practice where we can connect to the stillness that exists within us, independent of everything we have seen, heard, and learned. Being able to connect to and cultivate this silence within you is a crucial part of your evolutionary leadership, because this is where you withdraw your senses from the overstimulation of the world around you, envision a world of equality outside of the one we are currently experiencing, and connect to creative solutions to actualize that vision.

THINKING POINT: MINDSET

● What are the practices that enable you to cultivate a healthy mindset for your vision?

● What are the triggers that send you spiraling into catastrophic or fearful thinking? What are the warning signs that you have been triggered and what interventions can you use to catch yourself if you do start spiraling?

● What are your practices for cultivating consciousness and connecting to the silence within you?

Energy + Mindset

When we consider your energy and mindset together, there is one aspect that unites them: your nervous system.

The role that your nervous system plays in developing your leadership qualities is a vital one and is often overlooked. It is most relevant to you as an evolutionary leader for a very specific reason. For much of this book we have been asking how to lead from beyond fear and ignite an optimism about a different possible future: one of greater equality for all. In order to lead others out of fear, we need to have a basic understanding of how fear shows up in the nervous system and affects the way we see and respond to the world.

As humans, we are generally dominated by one particular state at a time. Either our sympathetic nervous system is leading, and we are in fight, flight, or freeze mode, or our parasympathetic nervous system is dominant, and we are in rest and digest. To keep it simple, we'll refer to these two branches of the nervous system as "stress response" and "calm response" from here on in.

You are probably already aware that if you are in a stress response, you see the world differently. Your mental state is more volatile, and it is easier to convince you of a catastrophic outcome. This is because the stress-based chemicals that are circulating in your body change the activity in the brain. You are sent into a part of your brain that used to be in charge before we evolved as humans and when we were more like reptiles. So basically, in our stress response, we are functioning more like a lizard than a human.

We need to be in our calm response to think and lead creatively. When we are in this state, the more conscious elements of our brain take over. We aren't simply a lizard reacting to our environment. We can tune into our consciousness and be more creative, dynamic, solution focused, and evolution orientated.

Our current social climate, the news, social media, television, the movies—all of these elements trigger us into a greater sense of fear than we were biologically designed to be in. When fear is triggered, it throws us into a stress response, changing our perspective and the way we view reality. This constant dance between our mind and our bodies is keeping us in a stress response, and from here, we are easier to control, market to, and manipulate.

Your role as an evolutionary thought leader is to first support your own nervous system to be in a calm response. This means choosing what you watch and read, who you associate with, how you show up in the world, as well as any practices you have such as meditation, yoga, working out at the gym, running, walking on the beach, etc. Then you can lead others from beyond fear, and model a different outcome based on your own practice.

Some people, like me, are more wired to be dominated by their stress response. Living in the heart of Manhattan, with an extremely sensitive nervous system, I do much to engineer a calm response. Besides a regular exercise program, I spend time meditating, carrying out deep breathing exercises, attending restorative yoga (a form of yoga where you lie in still positions for five minutes at a time to regulate the nervous system), doing cold therapy, and spending time in nature. I also avoid sugar, caffeine and other stimulants that throw me into a stress response and give me short bursts of energy that aren't sustained in the long term. Although I give high priority to the regulation of my calm response, not everyone needs to take the level of care that I do, and sometimes even a minor practice can enable the calm response to reset, and with it, the mindset and perspective.

THINKING POINT: What's the relationship between your nervous system and your thought patterns? How does your stress response mindset compare to your calm response mindset? What are the practices that take you into a calm state? How essential are these to you and what level of commitment is needed so that you are able to fundamentally lead from a calm response?

(iii) PRESENCE

Your presence can be summarized as how much compassion you have for yourself and others and how that compassion shows up in your work and wider life. It includes how you show up with:

- Yourself - including your self-esteem, confidence, thoughts that you have about yourself, how you take care of yourself, etc.
- Your partner / sexual or intimate partner(s) - how you respond to and communicate with those you get close with (whether you have a long-term partner or more casual connections)
- Your family - how you speak to and show up for those in your family circle
- Your friends - how you treat them and those in your "inner circle"

● Your audience or clients - how you treat those who follow you or have placed their trust in you. How you communicate with those who see the world the same as you as well as those who see the world differently from you

● Strangers - waiting staff, people in the supermarket, people on the street, etc.

There are a number of qualities that make up your presence. Are you here in the room when you are with people? Are you listening carefully to what they are saying? Do you have a script that you repeat to people or are you dynamically altering your communication in every moment? Do you have the patience to understand the different programming that others have received and work with it, even if it goes against what you believe to be true? Are you able to meet people where they are at and connect with them despite any differences you may have? These are the questions which will give you an insight into the kind of presence you have as a leader.

In Chapter 11 we talked about authenticity, and one of the biggest indicators of your legitimacy as a leader is how you treat those around you. Having worked in the self-growth and personal development industry for some years, I saw many examples of great leadership, alongside a fair deal of inauthenticity. A thought leader's message and their actions don't always match, and the biggest indicator of this is in their communication with others. If a leader had a message of love and unity, for example, then how was this showing up in their interactions with their children, when they passed a homeless person on the street, or when someone disagreed with their message? In the old paradigm of leadership, inconsistencies were accepted, but we are now dawning on a new era, where the old structures are breaking down and we are asking for more authenticity and truth in someone before we call them a leader. If we judge those in leadership roles as inconsistent, contrary or unpredictable, we have to be equally aware of our own characteristics that may conflict with our message, so we can ensure that we address them, evolve them, and model them to our audience as authentic leaders of change.

THINKING POINT: How do you show up with yourself / those closest to you / acquaintances / your audience / people who see the world like you / people who see the world differently from you / complete strangers? What are your blind spots with your presence with others and where do you need to work towards greater authenticity?

ENERGY AND PRACTICES = PRESENCE

Some aspects of presence are integral to our character while others can be developed. I often talk about presence in relation to energy and mindset, because when you have practices that generate your energy and develop your mindset and consciousness, they will greatly affect your presence. A leader who is focused on generating the energy for their mission through healthy eating, exercising and sleeping, who has mindfulness or meditation practices, who takes care of their nervous system to generate a calm response, and so on, is likely to have a dramatically different presence than one who runs on stimulants and junk food, and is in a constant stress response.

THINKING POINT: What are the practices that influence your presence? With your current practices (or any new ones that you undertake), notice how they affect your presence:

 (a) before
 (b) afterwards
 (c) later that day
 (d) in the long run

If you see each practice that you do as part of your evolutionary leadership, then every time you contribute to yourself, you will be contributing to your mission, and the outcome will be a much more grounded and self-regulated leader who has a greater influence on others.

CHAPTER SUMMARY

● You can have the most well-crafted message in history, but if you haven't considered how you show up to deliver it, you can fall short of making an impact.

● Three core interrelated pieces that affect you as the messenger: (i) energy, (ii) mindset, (iii) presence.

● However powerful your message is, your own vitality—the energy you have within you—is what will actually see your mission through.

● You can either generate, stagnate or deplete your energy. Your main focus as an evolutionary thought leader is on what generates your energy, with an awareness on what stagnates or depletes your energy too.

● Mindset includes your vision, your ability to navigate mental triggers, and cultivating consciousness.

● Your energy and your mindset are united by your nervous system.

● As humans, we are dominated by one particular branch of the nervous system at any given time—either sympathetic (we called this stress response), or parasympathetic (we called this calm response).

● We need to be in our calm response to think and lead creatively. When we are in this state, the more conscious elements of our brain take over.

● Your role as an evolutionary thought leader is to first support your own nervous system to be in a calm response. Then you can lead others from beyond fear, and model a different outcome based on your own practice.

● Your presence is how much compassion you have for yourself and others and how that compassion shows up with yourself / those closest to you / acquaintances / your audience / people who see the world like you / people who see the world differently from you / complete strangers.

● When you have practices that generate your energy and develop your mindset and consciousness, they will greatly affect your presence.

● If you see each practice that you do as part of your evolutionary leadership, then every time you contribute to yourself, you will be contributing to your mission.

Conclusion

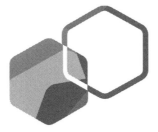

Whatever your individual message or area of passion is, there is one goal I'm hoping that we all share: to contribute to a greater experience of equality, peace, unity, and compassion for everyone. Each and every one of us can make a practical contribution to that goal and to shaping the kind of world that we want to live in. Every single act of social evolution, no matter how small, adds immense value to society's progression as a whole.

As an authentic messenger for social change you can't control how each individual perceives your message, and you definitely don't know how something you share is going to land. Yet each time you authentically share a message, it has the potential to contribute to breaking down prejudice, whether you cause someone to look within, stop and think or change their course of action. You may not always see the full extent of your impact, but your main goals are to stand true to your message, to keep refining and defining it as you grow yourself, and to constantly remind yourself of the kind of society you are leading others towards. Those goals are what will keep your audience moving towards actual, meaningful growth.

As you continue to address your role as an influencer what you share will expand on a multidimensional level. If you have heard the calling (the "why" of your message), found your audience (the "who" of your message), begun to craft a unique message (the "what" of your message), chosen your vehicle (the "how" of your message), and begun to shape yourself as an authentic and dynamic leader, you will realize by now that this is a complex process with many moving parts. You will need to address these elements over and over again as both you and what you are sharing continue to evolve.

If you get lost or unsure of the way forward at any time, it can help to ask yourself this simple question: "Is this contributing to change?" Building a bridge to your audience is at the forefront of effective communication. If you stay focused on the end result you are aiming for, then your actions will be aligned. You might need to disrupt, unite, call in, call out, or support to get there, but when you know what your purpose is, you can stay true under all circumstances. This will help you stand strong in your commitment to support humanity so that you can continue to make a practical and powerful contribution. By carefully crafting and delivering dynamic social messages you can truly become a catalyst of change.

Resources

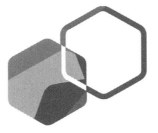

For all the links to the articles, speeches and video clips presented in this book, visit:

http://www.equalityhive.com/book-resources/

To find out more about working with Sasha Allenby and Equality Hive for ghostwriting and consultancy services, coaching programs, or to sign up for weekly blogs and updates, visit:

http://www.equalityhive.com

Acknowledgments

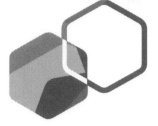

A huge thank you to my partner, Mammad Mahmoodi. Our daily conversations have fed everything that was written in this book. Your perspective on life continues to fire and inspire me in every moment. I'm sincerely blessed to have you in my life and am incredibly grateful for your love and support.

To Brett Moran, my "brother from another mother." Our valuable and supportive friendship is one of a kind. Our connection has been a gift since the day we met and many of my achievements over this past decade have been inspired by your encouragement and belief in me.

To Lois Rose for your skillful editing. You put your heart and soul into editing this book, and your careful and considerate input is always deeply appreciated—this time, and on every project we have worked on together.

To Emily Hutton for your invaluable assistance on research and your contribution to a variety of speeches, posts and articles in this book. Also for your keen eye for quality and your feedback on style and content.

Thanks to Brett Moran, Shamash Alidina, Ari Gold, Samy Nemir, Reva Patwardhan, Paul Zelizer, Katie Smith and Nick Jankel for your generous reviews of the book.

Thanks to David Harshada Wagner for helping me to define the term "social evolution."

End Notes

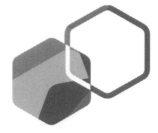

Chapter 1

i.   Howard Zinn, "The Optimism of Uncertainty," *Nation*, September 2, 2004, https://www.thenation.com/article/optimism-uncertainty/.

Chapter 2

i.   Nuccio DiNuzzo, Twitter post, January 30, 2017, 6:39 p.m. https://twitter.com/ChiTribNuccio/status/826258508274343940.

ii.   Eric Bradner, "NYC mayor: Trump travel ban 'sends a horrible message'," CNN, January 29, 2017, https://www.cnn.com/2017/01/29/politics/bill-de-blasio-trump-travel-ban/index.html.

Chapter 3

i.   Malala Yousafzai, quoted in Brian MacQuarrie, "Malala Yousafzai addresses Harvard audience," *The Boston Globe*, September 28, 2013, https://www.bostonglobe.com/metro/2013/09/27/malala-yousafzai-pakistani-teen-shot-taliban-tells-harvard-audience-that-education-right-for-all/6cZBan0M4J3cAnmRZLfUmI/story.html.

ii.   Eleanor Steafel, How Iran's brave women are fighting for right to ditch their hijabs, 9 Feb 2017, https://www.telegraph.co.uk/women/politics/irans-brave-women-fighting-right-ditch-hijabs/.

iii. Layla Saad, "I Need to Talk to Spiritual White Women About White Supremacy (Part Two)," *Wild Mystic Woman*, October 16, 2017, http://www.wildmysticwoman.com/poetry-prose/white-women-white-supremacy-2.

iv. John Branch, "The Awakening of Colin Kaepernick," *New York Times*, September 7, 2017, https://www.nytimes.com/2017/09/07/sports/colin-kaepernick-nfl-protests.html.

v. "About The Film," Accidental Courtesy, accessed July 7, 2017, https://accidentalcourtesy.com/about-the-film/.

vi. Lola Okolosie, "Emma Watson's willingness to face the truth about race is refreshing," *The Guardian*, January 10, 2018, https://www.theguardian.com/commentisfree/2018/jan/10/emma-watson-truth-race-white.

vii. Erin Canty, "People called Emma Watson a 'white feminist.' Now, she admits they weren't wrong," *Upworthy*, January 12, 2018, http://www.upworthy.com/people-called-emma-watson-a-white-feminist-now-she-admits-they-weren-t-wrong.

viii. "About," It Gets Better, accessed July 7, 2017, https://itgetsbetter.org/about/.

Chapter 4

i. Sandra E. Garcia, "The Woman Who Created #MeToo Long Before Hashtags," *New York Times*, October 20, 2017, https://www.nytimes.com/2017/10/20/us/me-too-movement-tarana-burke.html.

ii. CBS/AP, "More than 12M 'Me Too' Facebook posts, comments, reactions in 24 hours," CBSNews, October 17, 2017, https://www.cbsnews.com/news/metoo-more-than-12-million-facebook-posts-comments-reactions-24-hours/.

iii. Matt Kahn All For Love, "Surviving Your Family Dynamic – Matt Kahn," Youtube video, 1:11:48, February 26, 2018, https://www.youtube.com/watch?v=26oP5VXEyHg.

iv. Martin Luther King, Jr., "I Have A Dream," (speech, Washington, DC,

August 28, 1963), Archives, https://www.archives.gov/files/press/exhibits/dream-speech.pdf.

v.   Brandon Stanton, "Houses for Rohingya Refugees," Go Fund Me, created March 4, 2018, https://www.gofundme.com/houses4rohingya.

vi.   Humans of New York, "They didn't say a word. They just started firing into the air and lighting our houses on fire. [...]", Facebook, March 5, 2018, https://www.facebook.com/humansofnewyork/posts/2183710791703009.

vii.   Ibid.

viii.   Ruth Umoh, "This CEO went from selling drugs and in prison to working with celebrities on their fitness," *CNBC*, July 28, 2017, https://www.cnbc.com/2017/07/28/this-fitness-ceo-went-from-being-a-drug-dealer-to-training-celebrities-.html.

ix.   Allana Akhtar, "How Cardi B Escaped Poverty to Become the First Female Rapper in 19 Years to Top the Charts," *Money*, September 27, 2017, http://time.com/money/4959065/how-cardi-b-escaped-poverty-to-become-the-first-female-rapper-in-19-years-to-top-the-charts/.

x.   NowThis, "This Wrongfully Convicted Man Became A Lawyer," Facebook video, n.d., https://www.facebook.com/NowThisNews/videos/1363105197112934/%20-%20I%20need%20a%20better%20source%20for%20this%20video.

xi.   Martin Luther King, Jr., "I Have A Dream," (speech, Washington, DC, August 28, 1963), Archives, https://www.archives.gov/files/press/exhibits/dream-speech.pdf.

Chapter 6

i.   Katie Reilly, "Lessons for 2018 From One of America's Most Tumultuous Years," *Time*, December 19, 2017, http://time.com/5071384/1968-historic-lessons-for-2018/.

ii.   Max Roser and Esteban Ortiz-Ospina, "Global Extreme Poverty," *Our World in Data*, March 27, 2017, "https://ourworldindata.org/extreme-poverty.

iii.   Gillian B. White, "Inequality Between America's Rich and Poor Is at a 30-Year High," *Atlantic*, December 18, 2014, https://www.theatlantic.com/business/archive/2014/12/inequality-between-americas-rich-and-americas-poor-at-30-year-high/383866/.

iv.   David Gelles, "Want to Make Money Like a C.E.O.? Work for 275 Years," *New York Times*, May 25, 2018, https://mobile.nytimes.com/2018/05/25/business/highest-paid-ceos-2017.html.

v.   "Criminal Justice Fact Sheet," NAACP, accessed July 16, 2018, http://www.naacp.org/criminal-justice-fact-sheet/.

vi.   Joe Posner, "There are huge racial disparities in how US police use force," Vox, accessed July 16, 2018, https://www.vox.com/cards/police-brutality-shootings-us/us-police-racism.

vii.   May Bulman, "Number of homeless people sleeping on streets in England hits highest level on record," *Independent*, January 25, 2018, https://www.independent.co.uk/news/uk/home-news/homelessness-rough-sleepers-record-england-stats-homeless-people-2017-increase-a8177086.html.

viii.   "Basic Facts About Homelessness: New York City," *Coalition for the Homeless*, http://www.coalitionforthehomeless.org/basic-facts-about-homelessness-new-york-city/.

ix.   Tanza Loudenback, "In each of the top 10 richest places in the world, residents have a combined wealth of at least $1 trillion," *Business Insider*, February 15, 2018, http://www.businessinsider.com/richest-cities-in-the-world-new-york-city-2018-2.

x.   Leen Abdallah, "The Cost to End World Hunger," *Borgen Project*, February 15, 2015, https://borgenproject.org/the-cost-to-end-world-hunger/.

xi.   Jennifer Calfas, "The Richest People in the World," *Money*, March 6, 2018, http://time.com/money/4746795/richest-people-in-the-world/.

xii. Ibid.

xiii. Ibid.

xiv. Ibid.

xv. "Hunger and Poverty Facts," Feeding America, accessed July 16, 2018, http://www.feedingamerica.org/hunger-in-america/hunger-and-poverty-facts.html.

xvi. Adam Tschorn, "Americans just spent $60.59 billion on pets. A by-the-numbers look at our obsession," *Los Angeles Times,* June 20, 2015, http://www.latimes.com/style/pets/la-hm-pets-index-20150620-story.html.

xvii. Debbie Phillips-Donaldson, "Global pet care sales pass $100 billion for first time," *Pet Food Industry,* February 7, 2017, https://www.petfoodindustry.com/blogs/7-adventures-in-pet-food/post/6263-global-pet-care-sales-pass-100-billion-for-first-time.

xviii Chloe Sorvino, "Why The $445 Billion Beauty Industry Is A Gold Mine for Self-Made Women," *Forbes,* May 18, 2017, https://www.forbes.com/sites/chloesorvino/2017/05/18/self-made-women-wealth-beauty-gold-mine/#904fec32a3a5.

xix. "Global fashion industry statistics – International apparel," FashionUnited, accessed July 16, 2018, https://fashionunited.com/global-fashion-industry-statistics.

xx. Elizabeth Weise, "Cyber Monday: Biggest online shopping day in U.S. history pits Amazon vs. Walmart," *USAToday,* November 27, 2017, https://www.usatoday.com/story/tech/2017/11/27/cyber-mondays-still-got-it-840-million-spent-10-0-am/897831001/).

xxi. "Khums in Islam," All About Shi'as, accessed July 16, 2018, http://allaboutshias.com/khums-in-islam/.

xxii. "Rhonda Byrne's Biography," *The Secret,* accessed July 18, 2018, https://www.thesecret.tv/about/rhonda-byrnes-biography/.

Chapter 7

i.   Nara Schoenberg, "WGN anchor told a Muslim blogger that she didn't 'sound like an American.' Her response went viral," *Chicago Tribune*, February 21, 2018, http://www.chicagotribune.com/lifestyles/ct-life-muslim-blogger-viral-02212018-story.html.

ii. Afua Hirsch, "I've had enough of white people who try to deny my experience," *Guardian*, January 24, 2018, https://www.theguardian.com/commentisfree/2018/jan/24/white-people-tv-racism-afua-hirsch.

iii. Mohamed Omar, "Jagmeet Singh, NDP Leadership Hopeful, Masterfully Handles Heckler At Brampton Event," *Huffington Post*, September 7, 2017,

iv. https://www.huffingtonpost.ca/2017/09/07/jagmeet-singh-ndp-leadership-hopeful-masterfully-handles-heckler-at-brampton-event_a_23200426/.

v.   Ryan Maloney, "Jagmeet Singh Explains Why He Didn't Tell That Heckler He's Sikh, Not Muslim," *Huffington Post*, September 9, 2018, https://www.huffingtonpost.ca/2017/09/09/jagmeet-singh-explains-why-he-didn-t-tell-that-heckler-he-s-sikh-not-muslim_a_23203030/.

Chapter 8

i.   Emma González, "Emma Gonzalez's powerful March for Our Lives speech in full-video," *Guardian*, March 24, 2018, https://www.theguardian.com/us-news/video/2018/mar/24/emma-gonzalezs-powerful-march-for-our-lives-speech-in-full-video.

ii. Murica Today, "Russell Brand Destroys Immigration Debate," Facebook video, January 22, 2018, https://www.facebook.com/MuricaTodayNewsNetwork/videos/838474622998638/.

iii. Andrew Sullivan, "It Gets Better—But Not Through Politics," Big Think, n.d., https://bigthink.com/videos/it-gets-better-but-not-through-politics.

iv.   Valarie Kaur, "'Breathe! Push!' Watch this sikh activist's powerful prayer for America," *The Washington Post*, March 6, 2017, https://www.washingtonpost.com/news/acts-of-faith/wp/2017/03/06/breathe-push-watch-this-sikh-activists-powerful-prayer-for-america/.

v.   Van Jones, "Van Jones #LoveArmy: Building a Movement with Love + Power," Youtube video, https://www.youtube.com/watch?v=wrh87WieWEo.

vi.   NYC Mayor's Office, "NYC Mayor Bill de Blasio's Promise to ALL New Yorkers #AlwaysNYC," Youtube video, November 23, 2016, https://www.youtube.com/watch?v=WZwz5h-l6mI.

vii. Claire Zillman, "'I Am Sorry. We Are Sorry.' Read Prime Minister Justin Trudeau's Formal Apology to Canada's LGBTQ Community," *Fortune*, November 29, 2017, http://fortune.com/2017/11/29/justin-trudeau-lgbt-apology-full-transcript/.

Chapter 9

i.   *Star Trek: Deep Space Nine,* episode 13, "Far Beyond the Stars," performed by Avery Brooks, aired February 11, 1998, on UPN.

ii.   Dr. Venus Opal Reese, *The Black Woman Millionaire: A Revolutionary Act that DEFIES Impossible,* (CreateSpace Independent Publishing Platform, 2018), back cover.

iii. Lindsay King-Miller, *Ask a Queer Chick* (New York: PLUME, 2016), I.

iv.   Juno Dawson, *This Book Is Gay* (London: Hot Key, 2014), 4-5.

v.   Roxane Gay, *Bad Feminist* (New York: Harper Perennial, 2014), I.

vi.   Layla Saad, "I Need to Talk to Spiritual White Women About White Supremacy (Part One)," *Wild Mystic Woman*, August 15, 2017, http://www.wildmysticwoman.com/poetry-prose/white-women-white-supremacy-1.

vii. hooks, bell, *Feminism is for Everybody* (New York: Routledge, 2014), 4.

viii. Akwaeke Emezi, "Transition My surgeries were a bridge across realities, a spirit customizing its vessel to reflect its nature," *The Cut*, January 19, 2018, https://www.thecut.com/2018/01/writer-and-artist-akwaeke-emezi-gender-transition-and-ogbanje.html.

ix.   Buzzfeed UK Staff, "Here's a Powerful Letter to Parkland Students from the Survivors of Britain's Last School Massacre," *Buzzfeed News*, March 13, 2018, https://www.buzzfeed.com/buzzfeeduk/heres-a-powerful-letter-to-parkland-students-from-the?utm_term=.tdleokKMV#.kt27YvyeL.

x.   Firoozeh Dumas, *Funny in Farsi; A Memoir of Growing Up Iranian in America* (New York: Random House Trade Paperbacks, 2003), 12.

xi.   Melissa Fleming, "Book extract: *A Hope More Powerful Than the Sea*," *UNA-UK*, March 17, 2017, https://www.una.org.uk/book-extract-hope-more-powerful-sea.

Chapter 10

i.   Salman Rushdie, "1,000 Days 'Trapped Inside a Metaphor'," (speech, New York, NY, December 11, 1991), *New York Times*, https://www.nytimes.com/1991/12/12/nyregion/excerpts-from-rushdie-s-address-1000-days-trapped-inside-a-metaphor.html.

ii.   Michael Margolis, *Believe Me: Why Your Vision, Brand, and Leadership Need a Bigger Story* (New York: Get Stories Press, 2009), 33.

iii. Annette Simmons, "*The Story Factor: Inspiration, Influence, and Persuasion through the Art of Storytelling*," (New York: Hachette Book Group, 2009), 2.

About the Author

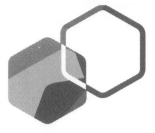

For the past decade, Sasha Allenby has been a ghostwriter for some of the greatest thought-leaders of our time. Her journey started when she co-authored a bestselling book that was published worldwide in twelve languages by industry giants, Hay House. Since then, Sasha has become a leading expert in crafting messages to impact change. She has ghostwritten over thirty books and is sought after globally for her work.

Since the 2016 elections, Sasha has focused on using her skill set to craft messages that support social equality. She lives in Manhattan with her partner, Mammad, where she takes an active role in contributing to social evolutionary issues.